Contents

What kind of bread exists?

Bread – an everyday staple for tons of meals that have been recorded throughout history as a prominent part of every cuisine and one of the first human-made foods. Over time, bread has gone through massive change, but with the same basic process. It is made with different kinds of flour and water and uses the process of baking.

Homemade bread is simple; it just needs flour, water, salt, yeast, baking soda, fat, and other ingredients to enhance or add more flavors such as herbs, spices, nuts, seeds, fruits, and vegetables. However, commercial bread has additional ingredients that improve its taste, nutrition, color, texture, and shelf life.

There are lots of kinds of bread. Why? Because bread is an essential part of our lives. Let's learn about the types of bread that exist and what makes them unique.

Arepa

A round and flat cornmeal patty baked, fried, or cooked on charcoal in Colombia and Venezuela. It is served with fillings like beans, ham, cheese, shredded beef, scrambled eggs, avocado, and chicken salad. To prepare arepa bread, you will need special corn flour, which is turned into a dough using a pinch of salt and water.

Baguette

A very popular French bread, a baguette is a long tube-like shaped bread with a soft interior and crunchy crust. Baguettes are used for preparing a variety of sandwiches.

Bagel

Originated in Poland, a bagel is now a famous bread in many parts of the world. This bread is first rolled, cooked in boiling water for a short time, and then baked. It comes in various flavors such as chocolate, raisin, cinnamon with added sugar, blueberry, onion, salmon, cheese, etc. They are a heart-healthy choice for a filling breakfast, a quick snack, or a delightful lunch.

Breadstick

Breadsticks are available in nearly every country in the world. A long and thin piece of bread baked for a long time makes a crispy breadstick. The baking time varies with the length of a breadstick.

Challah

Challah is a traditional Jewish bread. The dough is first braided and then baked, thus giving this bread a unique appearance. It is prepared with flour, yeast, honey, and eggs and has a sweet taste.

Chapati

Chapati is a famous bread in Asian regions such as India, Pakistan, Afghanistan, and Iran. They are made with wheat flour and toasted over a griddle pan instead of being baked. Chapati can be eaten as it is or with cooked vegetables and meat dishes and lentil soups. Although chapati is made without oil, they are sometimes buttered, such as parathas.

Ciabatta

Ciabatta is an Italian bread, and its crust and texture vary slightly throughout the regions of Italy. However, the essential ingredients are the same, wheat flour, yeast, salt, and water. Ciabatta is used for paninis and Italian sandwiches.

Cornbread

Cornbread is prepared with ground corn, egg, and buttermilk. Ground corn or cornmeal gives this dense and crumbly bread a cake-like taste and texture.

Croissant

A crescent moon-shaped a French roll that is incredibly buttery, flaky, and very rich. They are traditionally a breakfast pastry and, therefore, commonly served with coffee in many European countries.

Crackers

Small segments of baked bread make crackers. They are baked by preparing a mixture of flour, salt, and water. The main difference between crackers and bread is that crackers have no leavening agent. They come in countless flavors today and serve as an appetizer or a snack with dip.

Crouton

When a very crunchy bread is divided into small pieces, the pieces are called croutons. To make croutons super crunchy, you need to bake the dough twice. But before the second one, cut it into small cubes and season with spices and herbs. They are used to garnish salads and soups.

Damper

A bush bread cooked over hot coals (can also be baked). It is made with the basic ingredients for bread, such as flour, salt, water, baking soda, and sometimes milk. It is a traditional bread in Australia and is served with cooked and dried meat dishes and stews.

English Muffins

A small and round yeast-leavened bread prepared by toasting dough on a griddle pan. It is usually sliced horizontally, toasted, and served during teatime. It can also be spread with butter and make excellent breakfast sandwiches.

Focaccia

It's a no-knead flatbread. But don't take focaccia entirely as a flatbread because yeast is present in its dough, which causes it to rise slightly. It is rich in flavor and retained a lot of moisture as the bread is brushed with lots of oil before baking. And, after baking, focaccia is often seasoned with salt, olives, or seasoning.

Fruit bread

This bread has fruit as one of its ingredients. For example, the most popular is banana bread. It can also be prepared with dried fruits and nuts. Due to its sweet taste, this bread is much like a cake.

Hot cross bun

A hot cross bun is a sweet and small round roll that comes with a cross shape on top of the dough. It is made with yeast and raisins and garnished with icing after baking. It is a traditional bun and is served on the Christian's Good Friday.

Naan

It is a Middle Eastern leavened bread, mostly found in the south, west, and central Asian countries. It is similar to pita bread but without a picket and baked in a clay oven. Naan is served with extra toppings such as cheese, butter, minced meat, or spiced vegetables.

Paratha

Paratha is a layered flatbread, made by combining whole wheat flour, salt, water, or milk, and then frying in oil, butter, or clarified butter. It is popular in India, Pakistan, Singapore, Malaysia, and Burma. Parathas are often stuffed with spiced vegetables like potatoes, onion, cabbage, and eggs.

Rye bread

It is made from rye flour and bread flour. That's why this bread comes in a different density, amount of fiber, and colors from light to dark. And due to rye's flavor, this bread has stronger flavors than traditional whole wheat bread.

Scone

Scone is a quick bread that is dense and dry and has a hard crust. It is prepared from flour, sugar, baking soda, butter, eggs, and milk. This bread is often flavored with fruits like berries or raisins and is eaten with honey, butter, and cream.

Soda bread

It is a traditional bread in Ireland made with flour, salt, baking soda, and buttermilk. It is often flavored with raisins or nuts and is soft, leavened, and sweet.

Tortilla

It is a soft and thin bread used in many Mexican dishes such as burritos, tacos, enchiladas, and wraps. Tortilla bread is segmented into small pieces seasoned with salt and spices, then deep-fried or baked in an oven and served as tortilla chips.

Whole-Wheat Bread

This bread is made from the flour of wheat grains with germ and bran. Hence, unlike white bread, this bead has more fiber and nutrients per slice. It is an excellent choice of sandwiches.

How is bread formed?

Bread is made by baking a mixture of flour, salt, yeast, water, and other ingredients. The basic process is to form a dough or a stiff paste, followed by baking in an oven or griddle into a loaf.

The secret of making good bread is to ensure that dough made by any process is provided with enough space to relax and expand itself while it is rising. A sign of good dough is that when pulled, it stretches out. The dough must be elastic and have the strength to hold gases produced during fermentation and stable enough to retain its cell structure and shape.

When flour is mixed with water, two proteins, known as glutenin and gliadin, are formed, which gives dough special features of elasticity and holding its shape. Gluten is also essential because it influences the mixing of dough ingredients, kneading, and baking properties of the loaf. Therefore, you should learn the correct way of mixing the ingredients for the dough.

Here is an overview of the steps for bread making.

· *Mixing the ingredients*

Mixing in breadmaking means even distribution of the various ingredients for the dough. The ingredients need to be mixed so the gluten can be developed, which gives the best result for bread. The mixing time of dough depends on the flour and the preferred mixing method, such as stirring, whisking, or processing ingredients in a blender. However, please don't mix the ingredients too much as in this way, the dough reduces its elastic properties. Similarly, undermixing the ingredients will cause an uneven rise in the bread that will give a poor appearance to the loaf from inside.

· *Fermentation*

When the ingredients of dough are mixed, they can be left for fermentation or rise. Fermentation is a slow process, and hence, dough changes its appearance slowly, usually 1 to 2 hours. The dough's appearance will tell about the fermentation. Like if the dough is a rough, dense mass, then fermentation is not doing its work. An extensible and smooth dough means everything is going just right.

So, how does the dough rise? The yeast grows by using sugar, the protein pieces (gluten) form a network, and carbohydrates (sugar) in the flour is breakdown into alcohol and carbon dioxide. This process is alcoholic fermentation. Carbon dioxide causes the dough to rise, and most of the alcohol evaporates during the baking process.

Heat also affects the rate of fermentation. As the temperature rises, the fermentation increase, and so does the production of carbon dioxide gas that expands the dough.

· *Kneading*

Kneading is needed to release any large gas formed during the fermentation or evenly distribute gas and temperature in the dough.

After kneading, the dough may rise again, if required by the recipe.

· *Baking*

Baking is a cooking procedure that transforms dough into a flavorful, soft, light, and digestible product. When the heat penetrates the dough during baking, the gases in the dough expand to increase the dough's size. The oven heat also evaporates alcohol by changing it into gas.

Until the dough temperature reaches 115 degrees F (46 degrees C), the dough keeps expanding. At 115 degrees F, the yeast dies, and no more sugar is consumed by yeast to produce carbon dioxide. The bread stops rising, and the remaining sugar in the dough is used to sweeten the loaf.

As the baking continues, the evaporation starts and the dough loses its moisture. The crust of the dough heats up and eventually reaches the temperature of the oven. Some of the protein (gluten) breaks down and gives an attractive brown color to the crust.

· *Cooling*

The bread is cooled when all the steam from the loaf is completely given off. When the loaf is cooled, it is wrapped or cut into slices to store or serve with food.

Ingredients

Flour

Wheat is grown in almost every part of the world. When wheat grains are ripe, they are harvested and milled into flour. A different variety of wheat produces a different range of flour in terms of fiber, protein, and gluten. Therefore, to bake perfect bread, the quality of flour is significant as its quality impacts the finished product.

For breadmaking, flour is moistened with water or milk, beaten, stirred, or kneaded to develop a stretched dough. The elasticity of the dough is essential to hold the gas produced during the fermentation of yeast.

Salt

Salt is a seasoning agent used to give taste to the bread. It is added in a very small amount in the bread mixture. Salt also helps in fermentation and strengthens the gluten, which produces bread with good texture and volume.

Yeast

Yeast is a leavening agent in bread. When provided with the right water, temperature, and food to grow, it releases carbon dioxide, increasing the dough's volume. It also expands the dough's cellular network, which forms bread crumbs and gives bread its unique aroma and flavor.

Water

Water is used to convert dry ingredients for bread into a dough. Adding the right amount of water in the dry mixture of dough is very important because it affects other dough ingredients' dispersal.

The many methods of creating bread

Straight Dough Method

Place all the ingredients in a large bowl, mix them, and leave the dough in a warm place for fermentation for a predetermined time. For the straight dough method, the time for fermentation depends on the type of the flour. If you are using flours that require two to three hours of fermentation time, then use the straight dough method to prep the dough. This method is not for those flour that needs a very long fermentation period as temperature may fluctuate that will cause acidic flavor and taste in the loaf.

No Time Dough Method

This method allows fermentation of dough for a brief period, about 30 minutes after mixing. Since this is not enough time for the yeast to produce enough gas to rise dough, yeast in no time dough method recipes is doubled or tripled the original quantity. The dough is made a little slacker and placed in a warmer place.

Salt Delayed Method

This method is similar to the straight dough method with a slight difference. All the ingredients are mixed to prepare the dough except for fat and salt. Salt has a controlling effect on the action of yeast. Fermentation is speedier in the dough without salt. Therefore, salt is added to the dough at the later stage or mixed in the dough after creamed in fat.

Tools for baking bread

1. Baking pans
Purchase baking pans in different shapes to give a specific shape to loaves.

2. Loaf pan
Loaf pans are made of disposable aluminum foil, heavy-gauge aluminum, ceramic material, or Pyrex glass. It comes in a rectangle shape.

3. Baking sheet
You will need a few baking sheets in different sizes, depending on the dough's size and the size of the oven. Purchase baking sheets that won't warp at high temperatures, such as gauge aluminum or steel. Standard sizes of baking sheets are 10.5 by 15 inches with a raised 1-inch edge, half baking sheet, and quarter sheet pan.

4. Bread mills
You enjoy fresh flour in your bread by milling wheat in your bread mill.

5. Cooling rack
A wire cooling rack helps in cooling down the bread properly after baking is done. Purchase the one that has short legs and allow adequate circulation.

6. Food processor or stand mixer
Although the preferable way to mix ingredients for the dough is by hand, it can be messy. Plus, it is difficult to work with sticky hands. Therefore, if you are baking regularly, combine ingredients in a food processor or stand mixer with a dough hook. These machines make the mixing process more manageable, and they are reliable to turn out an edible dough.

7. Knives
A sharp knife can make cuts on the dough, such as in hot cross buns. Also, pur-

chase a serrated knife for slicing the bread. Always cut bread on a cutting board to cut the loaf with no damage to the blade.

8. Measuring cups and spoons

You must have cups and spoons for accurate measurement of the dry and wet ingredients for the dough. A long wooden spoon will also work in place of plastic spoons. Purchase clear liquid measuring cups that come with a spout to pour liquid ingredients accurately.

9. Mixing bowls

You must have a sturdy large bowl, about 4-quarts, on hand to mix your ingredients. Use a plastic or ceramic bowl in various sizes for mixing.

10. Plastic spatula

This tool will help in removing stuck dough on the inside of the bowl or bread machine pans. You can also use a spatula to transfer dough by lifting it.

11. Plastic wrap/kitchen towel

A plastic wrap or a linen kitchen towel is used while the dough is expanding. The kitchen towel should be damp, not moist, and plastic wrap should be sprayed with oil.

12. Parchment paper

Parchment paper is used to line baking pans and loaf pans before adding dough in it as it cuts down cleaning the baking and loaf pans. Grease parchment paper when using.

13. Pastry brushes

Pastry brushes are used to grease dough with oil or butter or applying glazes. A silicone pastry brush works best, and it is easy to clean.

14. Pastry board

If your kitchen counter is not good enough to roll the dough, you can consider a pastry board for this job. It is made of bamboo, wood, or marble. Purchase the pastry board that can lock to your working table or kitchen counter.

15. Rolling pin
A rolling pin helps in rolling and shaping the dough in appropriate shape and thickness.

16. Silicone mat
If you are frustrated with cutting the parchment paper to the right size for baking, you can use a silicon mat as an alternative. They come in sizes of half and full sheet baking trays and are reusable and easy to clean. They also prevent sticking of baking items to the tray.

17. Timer
Timing is everything in bread baking. A timer will let you relax throughout the baking process and will indicate when the dough is ready. So, with the timer, you don't have to keep an eye on the clock continuously for noting the time and monitor the progress of dough.

18. Thermometer
Temperature is a significant factor when baking bread with yeast. You must know the water's accurate temperature and the environment to achieve the best result of fermentation. For this, purchase a quality digital probe thermometer or a long-stemmed instant-read yeast thermometer.

19. Whisker
A whisker is a convenient tool in mixing ingredients. Use a stainless steel or silicone wire whiskers with a long handle when making bread.

What do you need to know before you start baking bread?

Making bread is a craft, but you don't have to be a professional in baking before testing your bread baking skills. Bread making is so simple that anyone can do it, and on the other hand, so complicated that you can take a lifetime in learning to make good bread. However, the only way to learn is to get your hands in the dough.

Step 1: Start with simple ingredients

Making bread is chemistry; therefore, you need a specific ratio of ingredients to make a soft and chewy bread. Start with making a simple white loaf because it is the easiest bread you can complete successfully. Once you get expert in the baking of a white loaf and get the hang of things, then experiment with a little more complicated ingredients for the dough.

Step 2: Know your ingredients

Don't assume flour as a flour. Flour comes in different types, with a range of proteins and gluten, which gives bread its unique properties. If the recipe doesn't state the kind of flour, then start with all-purpose flour.

Yeast is another key ingredient in bread making. Make sure you are using the right type of yeast in your dough; it will be instant yeast or active dry yeast. Also, store yeast in the refrigerator or freezer to keep it fresh. When you want it alive, treat it gently with warm water and let it emulsify slightly before adding into the flour.

Step 3: Equip your Kitchen

Before you start preparing dough for the loaf, you must make sure that every necessary tool for this process is available to you to get things to work in order and quickly. Read the section 'Tools for baking bread' to know more about the breadmaking tools.

Step 4: Understand the basics of baking

Making bread requires five simple steps: Mixing, fermentation, kneading, baking, and cooling. Read the section 'How is bread formed?' to learn details of each step.

Step 5: Learn when it's ready

Baking bread is not about putting it in the oven until it gets a nice deep brown color on top. No, you have to know if your loaf is ready or not. For this, you must prepare the dough by following accurate ingredients amount, temperature, and time specified in the recipe. This is followed by baking in the preheated oven and then checking the bread with a toothpick or knife test. If your bread smells like toast, has a deep golden-brown color, and a knife slid into the loaf comes out clean, the loaf of bread is ready. If it sounds hollow, then the bread is thoroughly cooked.

Don't just give up at the first time. Making good bread takes lots of patience and practice. And, over time, you will learn how and when to adjust the recipe and make the dough with the right consistency. Have faith in your kitchen skills, and one day, you will hone the excellent bread baking craft.

Zucchini Cheddar Bread

If you have got some zucchini and some chunks of cheese in your refrigerator, use these ingredients to make this deliciously easy cheesy bread.

Prep Time:	15 minutes	Calories:	269
Cook Time:	60 minutes	Fat (g):	13
Total Time:	1h 15 m	Protein (g):	10
Servings:	8	Carbs:	27

Ingredients:

• Zucchini, grated	1 ½ cups
• All-purpose flour	2 cups
• Baking powder	2 teaspoons
• Baking soda	½ teaspoon
• Salt	½ teaspoon
• Milk, non-fat, unsweetened	1 cup
• Egg, at room temperature	1
• Butter, unsalted	3 tablespoons
• Cheddar cheese, grated	1 ½ cups
• Green onion, chopped	2

Instructions:

1. Switch on the oven, then set it to 350 degrees F (177°C) and let it preheat.
2. Meanwhile, take a 9-by-5 inches bread pan, grease it with oil and set it aside until required.
3. Take a paper towel or a kitchen towel, wrap zucchini in it and squeeze well to remove excess liquid from it.
4. Take a large bowl, place flour in it, add salt, baking powder, and soda, and then stir until mixed.
5. Take a small bowl, pour in the milk, and whisk in milk until a slightly curdle mixture comes together and then whisk in egg and butter until combined.
6. Pour milk mixture into the flour mixture, whisk until incorporated, and then fold in green onions, zucchini, and cheese until just mixed and smooth batter for dough comes together.
7. Spoon the dough into the prepared bread pan and then bake for 60 minutes or more until the crust turned golden brown and passes the toothpick test; a toothpick should come out clean from the pan or else continue baking for another 10 minutes.
8. When done, let the bread cool in its pan for 10 minutes, then carefully lift out the bread, and transfer it to a wire rack for 1 hour or more until cooled.
9. Cut bread into eight slices and then serve.

Cheese Bread

This cheese bread is ridiculously easy to make. For more flavors, you may add sundried tomatoes, olives, or onions. Bake it this holiday, and all of your family will love it.

Prep Time:	15 minutes	Calories:	222
Cook Time:	40 minutes	Fat (g):	10
Total Time:	55 minutes	Protein (g):	9
Servings:	12	Carbs:	24

Ingredients:

- All-purpose flour   2 cups
- Baking powder   4 teaspoons
- Sugar   1 tablespoon
- Salt   ½ teaspoon
- Shredded cheddar cheese   1 ¼ cups
- Milk   1 cup
- Egg, at room temperature   1
- Olive oil   2 tablespoons
- Mustard paste   1 teaspoon
- Olives, chopped   ¾ cup
- Ground black pepper   ¾ teaspoon
- Dried rosemary   ½ teaspoon

Instructions:

1. Switch on the oven, then set it to 375 degrees F (190°C) and let it preheat.
2. Meanwhile, take a 9-by-5 inches bread pan, grease it with oil and set it aside until required.
3. Take a large bowl, place flour in it, add sugar, salt, black pepper, rosemary, and baking powder and then stir until combined.
4. Add the shredded cheese and mix everything well.
5. Take a medium bowl, crack the egg in it, add oil and mustard, pour in the milk, and whisk until blended.
6. Pour the egg mixture into the flour mixture, whisk until incorporated, and then fold in olives until just mixed.
7. Spoon the dough into the prepared bread pan and then bake for 40 minutes or more until the crust turned golden brown and passes the toothpick test; a toothpick should come out clean from the pan or else continue baking for another 10 minutes.
8. When done, let the bread cool in its pan for 10 minutes, then carefully lift out the bread, and transfer it to a wire rack for 1 hour or more until cooled.
9. Cut bread into twelve slices and then serve.

Swiss Beer Bread

Prep Time:	15 minutes	Calories:	182
Cook Time:	60 minutes	Fat (g):	5
Total Time:	1h 15 m	Protein (g):	6
Servings:	12	Carbs:	28

Ingredients:

• Swiss cheese	4 oz (113 g)
• All-purpose flour	3 cups
• Sugar	3 tablespoons
• Baking powder	3 teaspoons
• Salt	1 ½ teaspoons
• Ground black pepper	½ teaspoon
• Beer, non-alcoholic	12 oz (340 g)
• Butter, unsalted, melted	2 tablespoons

Instructions:

1. Switch on the oven, then set it to 375 degrees F (190°C) and let it preheat.
2. Meanwhile, take a 9-by-5 inches bread pan, grease it with butter and set it aside until required.
3. Divide the Swiss cheese in half, shred one half of the cheese, and then cut the remaining half of cheese into ¼-inch cubes.
4. Take a large bowl, place flour in it, add salt, sugar, black pepper, and baking powder and then stir until mixed.
5. Pour in beer, whisk until incorporated and smooth batter comes together and then fold in grated and cubed cheese until mixed.
6. Spoon the dough into the prepared bread pan and then bake for 60 minutes or more until the crust turned golden brown and passes the toothpick test; a toothpick should come out clean from the pan or else continue baking for another 10 minutes.
7. When done, let the bread cool in its pan for 10 minutes, then carefully lift out the bread, and transfer it to a wire rack for 1 hour or more until cooled.
8. Cut bread into twelve slices and then serve.

Apple Cider Bread

Treat yourself this fall with this delicious apple cider bread. It is sweetened only with honey. And, it goes great for a breakfast or snack.

Prep Time:	15 minutes	Calories:	211
Cook Time:	45 minutes	Fat (g):	8
Total Time:	60 minutes	Protein (g):	5
Servings:	10	Carbs:	31

Ingredients:

• Oat flour	2 cups
• Baking powder	1 teaspoon
• Baking soda	1 teaspoon
• Ground cinnamon	1 ½ teaspoons
• Ground ginger	½ teaspoon
• Ground nutmeg	¼ teaspoon
• Coconut oil, melted, cooled	¼ cup
• Egg, at room temperature	1
• Egg white, at room temperature	1
• Vanilla extract, unsweetened	1 teaspoon
• Honey	1/3 cup
• Applesauce	¾ cup
• Apple cider	¾ cup
• Apples, peeled, chopped	1 cup

Instructions:

1. Switch on the oven, then set it to 350 degrees F (177°C) and let it preheat.
2. Meanwhile, take a 9-by-5 inches bread pan, grease it with oil and set it aside until required.
3. Take a large bowl, place flour in it, add cinnamon, ginger, nutmeg, baking powder, and soda, and then stir until mixed.
4. Take a medium bowl, crack the egg in it, add egg white, pour in oil, vanilla, honey, apple cider, and apple sauce and whisk until blended.
5. Pour egg mixture into the flour mixture until incorporated and then fold in apple pieces until just mixed.
6. Spoon the dough into the prepared bread pan and then bake for 45 minutes or more until the crust turned golden brown and passes the toothpick test; a toothpick should come out clean from the pan or else continue baking for another 10 minutes.
7. When done, let the bread cool in its pan for 10 minutes, then carefully lift out the bread, and transfer it to a wire rack for 1 hour or more until cooled.
8. Cut bread into ten slices and then serve.

Gouda and Roasted Potato Bread

Incorporate potatoes into your regular bread recipe and make a loaf of delicious potato bread.
Also, flavoring it with smoked gouda cheese will take the taste and texture to a new level.

Prep Time:	1 h 55 m	Calories:	101
Cook Time:	60 minutes	Fat (g):	2
Total Time:	2 h 55 m	Protein (g):	3
Servings:	16	Carbs:	18

Ingredients:

- Potatoes, peeled, chopped   8 oz (227 g)
- All-purpose flour   3 cups
- Yeast, active, dry   ¼ oz (7 g)
- Salt   1 ½ teaspoons

- Smoked gouda cheese, shredded   ½ cup
- Olive oil   1 ½ teaspoons
- Water, at 120 degrees F   1 cup

Instructions:

1. Switch on the oven, set the baking rack in the middle section, then set it to 425 degrees F (218°C) and let it preheat. Take 15-by-10 inches baking pan, grease it with oil, spread chopped potatoes on it, and then drizzle with oil.
2. Season potatoes with ½ teaspoon of salt, toss until coated and roast for 25 minutes until tender, stirring frequently.
3. Then take a large bowl, place 2 cups of flour in it, add 1 teaspoon of salt and then whisk in water by using an electric beater until smooth batter comes together.
4. Stir in enough remaining flour until the dough comes sticky, then spoon the dough onto a cleaned and dusted surface and knead it for 8 minutes.
5. Knead in cheese and roasted potatoes, spoon the dough into a bowl greased with oil, then grease the top, cover it with a plastic wrap and let it rest for 1 hour until the dough doubled. Then spoon the dough onto a clean working space dusted with flour, punch it down and then shape it into a 7-inch round loaf.
6. Take a baking sheet, line it with parchment paper, place the prepared loaf on it, cover it with a kitchen towel, and let it rest into a warm place for 45 minutes until dough expands.
7. Meanwhile, switch the temperature of the oven to 375 degrees F (190°C), take a heatproof skillet pan on the bottom rack of the oven and let it preheat.
8. Take a tea kettle, pour in 2 cups of water, and then bring it to a boil.
9. When the dough has expanded, make some ¼-inch deep cuts onto the top of the dough by using a sharp knife and then transfer it carefully on the top rack of the oven.
10. Pour boiling water into the skillet pan, return it into the oven, and let the dough bake for 35 minutes until the crust turned golden brown and passes the toothpick test; a toothpick should come out clean from the pan or else continue baking for another 10 minutes.
11. When done, let the bread cool in its pan for 10 minutes, then carefully lift out the bread, and transfer it to a wire rack for 1 hour or more until cooled.
12. Cut bread into sixteen slices and then serve.

Oatmeal Sandwich Bread

If you are a novice in baking bread, then this oatmeal sandwich bread can help you proficient your skills. Its exterior is crunchy, and the interior is fluffy and soft. It makes a great jelly and peanut butter sandwiches.

Prep Time:	3 hours	Calories:	140
Cook Time:	45 minutes	Fat (g):	2
Total Time:	3 h 45 m	Protein (g):	6
Servings:	8	Carbs:	26

Ingredients:

- All-purpose flour   3 cups
- Oats, old-fashion   ½ cup + ¼ cup
- Sugar   1 tablespoon
- Yeast, active, dry   ½ teaspoon
- Butter, unsalted, softened   1 tablespoon
- Salt   ½ tablespoon
- Water, warm   1 1/3 cup

Instructions:

1. Take a large bowl, add yeast in it along with a pinch of sugar, pour in water, stir and let it rest for 10 minutes at a warm place until emulsified.
2. Then add flour, ½ cup of oats, sugar, salt, and butter and whisk by using an electric beater until a smooth dough comes together.
3. Cover the bowl containing dough with a plastic wrap and then let it rest for 1 hour to 1 hour and 30 minutes until the dough doubled in size.
4. Then spoon the dough onto a clean working space dusted with the flour, punch it down, knead it for 5 minutes, then cover the dough with a kitchen towel and let it rest for 20 minutes.
5. After 20 minutes, form the dough into a small log and roll in the remaining oats.
6. Place it into a loaf pan greased with oil, then cover it with a kitchen towel and let it rest for 45 minutes at a warm place.
7. Meanwhile, switch on the oven, then set it to 375 degrees F (190°C) and let it preheat.
8. When ready to bake, place the loaf pan in it and then bake for 45 minutes until the crust turned golden brown and passes the toothpick test; a toothpick should come out clean from the pan.
9. When done, turn the pan upside down to take out the bread and then transfer it to a wire rack for 30 minutes or more until cooled.
10. Cut bread into eight slices and then serve.

Olive Focaccia

This recipe presents olives and tomatoes into the regular focaccia recipe. It's a delectable and scrumptious accompaniment to any meal.

Prep Time:	1h 25 m	Calories:	118
Cook Time:	18 minutes	Fat (g):	3
Total Time:	1h 43 m	Protein (g):	3
Servings:	8	Carbs:	19

Ingredients:

- Yeast, active, dry   1 1/8 teaspoons
- Water, at 115 degrees F   ½ cup
- Sugar   1 tablespoon
- Italian seasoning   1 tablespoon
- Salt   ¼ teaspoon

• Ground black pepper	¼ teaspoon
• All-purpose flour	1 2/3 cups
• Tomatoes, sliced	3 oz (85 g)
• Sliced olives	4 tablespoons
• Minced rosemary	1 tablespoon
• Olive oil	1 tablespoon
• Salt	1 teaspoon
• Parmesan cheese, shredded	1 teaspoon
• Romano cheese, shredded	1 teaspoon

Instructions:

1. Take a large bowl, add yeast in it along with a pinch of sugar, pour in water, stir and let it rest for 10 minutes at a warm place until emulsified.

2. Then add flour along with salt, black pepper, sugar, and Italian seasoning and whisk by using an electric beater until a smooth dough comes together.

3. Spoon the dough onto a clean working space dusted with flour and then knead for 8 minutes until elastic.

4. Take a large bowl, grease it with oil, place prepared dough in it, grease the top with oil, cover the bowl with a kitchen towel and let it rest for 50 minutes at a warm place until doubled in size.

5. Then punch the dough to remove the air bubbles as much as possible, shape it into a 9-inch round, and place onto a baking sheet greased with oil.

6. Cover the dough with a kitchen towel and then let it rest for 25 minutes until doubled in size. Meanwhile, switch on the oven, then set it to 400 degrees F (204°C) and let it preheat.

7. When the dough has raised, spread the olives and tomatoes, then pressing them slightly into the dough; brush the dough with oil and sprinkle with salt, rosemary, and cheeses.

8. Bake the bread for 18 minutes or more until the crust turned golden brown and passes the toothpick test; a toothpick should come out clean from the pan or else continue baking for another 10 minutes.

9. When done, transfer the bread to a wire rack for 1 hour or more until cooled.

10. Cut bread into eight slices and then serve.

Jalapeno Buttermilk Cornbread

This cornbread is the next level bread. It is sweet, savory, and spicy, offering a touch of buttermilk, honey, and jalapeno peppers.

Prep Time:	15 minutes	Calories:	180
Cook Time:	25 minutes	Fat (g):	4
Total Time:	40 minutes	Protein (g):	6
Servings:	8	Carbs:	32

Ingredients:

- All-purpose flour   1 cup
- Cornmeal   1 cup
- Buttermilk   1 cup
- Egg, at room temperature   1
- Olive oil, divided   3 tablespoons
- Honey   2 tablespoons
- Mayonnaise   1 tablespoon
- Corn, fresh or frozen   ¼ cup
- Jalapeno pepper, deseeded, chopped   1

Instructions:

1. Switch on the oven, then set it to 425 degrees F (218°C) and let it preheat.
2. Meanwhile, take an 8-inch skillet pan, grease it with 1 tablespoon of oil and set it aside until required.
3. Take a large bowl, place flour in it, add cornmeal and then stir until mixed.
4. Take a medium bowl, crack the egg in it, add the remaining 2 tablespoons of oil, mayonnaise, and honey, pour in the buttermilk and whisk until well combined.
5. Transfer the egg mixture into the mixture of flour, whisk by using an electric beater until smooth, and then fold in cheese, corn, and jalapeno pepper until just mixed.
6. Pour the batter into the skillet pan and then bake for 20 to 25 minutes or more until the crust turned golden brown and passes the toothpick test; a toothpick should come out clean from the pan or else continue baking for another 10 minutes.
7. When done, let the bread cool in its pan for 10 minutes, then cut bread into eight slices and then serve.

Spiced Pumpkin Bread

This sweet and spicy pumpkin bread is hard to beat!

Prep Time:	15 minutes	Calories:	166
Cook Time:	1h 5 m	Fat (g):	6
Total Time:	1h 20 m	Protein (g):	2
Servings:	12	Carbs:	26

Ingredients:

- All-purpose flour   1 cup
- Salt   ¼ teaspoon
- Baking soda   ½ teaspoon
- Baking powder   ¼ teaspoon
- Ground cloves   ½ teaspoon
- Ground cinnamon   ½ teaspoon
- Ground nutmeg   ½ teaspoon
- Butter, unsalted, softened   6 tablespoons
- Sugar   1 cup
- Egg, at room temperature   1
- Pumpkin puree   7.5 oz (213 g)

Instructions:

1. Switch on the oven, then set it to 325 degrees F (163°C) and let it preheat.
2. Meanwhile, take an 8-by-4 inches bread pan, grease it with oil and set it aside until required.
3. Take a medium bowl, place flour in it, add all the spices, salt, baking powder, and soda and then stir until mixed.
4. Take a large bowl, place butter in it, whisk in the sugar by using an electric beater until creamy, and then beat in the egg until fluffy.
5. Beat in pumpkin puree until combined and gradually beat in flour mixture until incorporated and the smooth batter comes together.
6. Transfer the batter into the prepared bread pan and then bake for 65 to 75 minutes or more until the crust turned golden brown and passes the toothpick test; a toothpick should come out clean from the pan or else continue baking for another 10 minutes.
7. When done, let the bread cool in its pan for 10 minutes, then carefully lift out the bread, and transfer it to a wire rack for 1 hour or more until cooled.
8. Cut bread into twelve slices and then serve.

Herb Bread

Bake this bread to complete a meal comprising of soups and stews. But the slices of this savory bread are so tasty that they go great alongside green salads. It's a treat for any time of the year.

Prep Time:	15 minutes	Calories:	147
Cook Time:	50 minutes	Fat (g):	5
Total Time:	1h 5 m	Protein (g):	3
Servings:	16	Carbs:	21

Ingredients:

• All-purpose flour	3 cups
• Sugar	3 tablespoons
• Baking powder	1 tablespoon
• Caraway seeds	3 teaspoons
• Salt	½ teaspoon
• Ground nutmeg	½ teaspoon
• Dried thyme	½ teaspoon
• Egg, at room temperature	1
• Milk	1 cup
• Olive oil	1/3 cup

Instructions:

1. Switch on the oven, then set it to 375 degrees F (190°C) and let it preheat.
2. Meanwhile, take a 9-by-5 inches bread pan, grease it with oil and set it aside until required.
3. Take a medium bowl, crack the egg in it and then beat in milk and oil by using an electric beater until smooth.
4. Take a large bowl, place flour in it, add remaining ingredients, stir until mixed.
5. Beat in the egg mixture into the flour mixture until incorporated.
6. Spoon the mixture into the prepared bread pan and then bake for 50 minutes or more until the crust turned golden brown and passes the toothpick test; a toothpick should come out clean from the pan or else continue baking for another 10 minutes.
7. When done, let the bread cool in its pan for 10 minutes, then carefully lift out the bread, and transfer it to a wire rack for 1 hour or more until cooled.
8. Cut bread into sixteen slices and then serve.

Salami Bread

If you are a salami pizza lover, then you must try this bread.

Prep Time:	2h	Calories:	214
Cook Time:	45 minutes	Fat (g):	8
Total Time:	2 h 45 m	Protein (g):	8
Servings:	12	Carbs:	26

Ingredients:

- Milk   1 ¼ cups
- Butter, unsalted, softened   1 ½ tablespoons
- Flour   3 cups

- Yeast, dry, active   ¼ oz (7 g)
- Sugar   1 tablespoon
- Salt   1 teaspoon
- Garlic powder   ½ teaspoon
- Salami, chopped   8 oz (227 g)

Instructions:

1. Take a 9-by-5 inches bread pan, grease it with oil, and set it aside until required.
2. Meanwhile, take a large bowl, place half of the flour in it, add salami, garlic powder, yeast, salt, and sugar and then whisk in butter and milk until well combined.
3. Knead the dough for 3 minutes and then knead in remaining flour, ½ cup at a time, until incorporated.
4. Take a separate large bowl, grease it with oil, place prepared dough in it, brush the top with oil, cover the bowl with a kitchen towel and let it rest for 1 hour at a warm place until double in size.
5. Then punch down the dough, cover it again with a kitchen towel and let it rest for 10 minutes.
6. Shape the dough, transfer it into the prepared pan, cover it with a plastic wrap, and let it rest for 45 minutes until risen.
7. Meanwhile, switch on the oven, then set it to 375 degrees F (190°C) and let it preheat.
8. Bake the bread for 10 minutes, then switch the temperature of the oven to 350 degrees F (177°C) and continue baking for another 35 minutes or more until the crust turned golden brown and passes the toothpick test; a toothpick should come out clean from the pan.
9. When done, let the bread cool in the bread pan for 10 minutes.
10. Then carefully lift out the bread, and transfer it to a wire rack for 1 hour or more until cooled.
11. Cut bread into twelve slices and then serve.

Cheddar and Chiles Bread

This delightful loaf is loaded with cheddar cheese and bits of green chilies. It goes great with soups and scrumptious bean dishes, and also very appealing as sandwich bread.

Prep Time:	20 h 30 m	Calories:	140
Cook Time:	60 minutes	Fat (g):	2
Total Time:	21 h 30 m	Protein (g):	5
Servings:	12	Carbs:	24

Ingredients:

- Bread flour   3 ½ cups
- Sugar   1 tablespoon
- Salt   1 ½ teaspoons

- Yeast, active, dry   1 teaspoon
- Olive oil   2 tablespoons
- Water, ice-cold   1 2/3 cups
- Cheddar cheese, grated   8 oz (227 g)
- Chopped green chilies   ½ cup

Instructions:

1. Take a medium bowl, place flour in it, add salt, sugar, and yeast and stir until mixed.
2. Take a large bowl, pour in water, whisk in oil and then whisk in flour mixture, ½ cup at a time, until incorporated.
3. Brush the top of the dough with oil, cover the bowl with a plastic wrap and then let it rest for a minimum of 3 hours or 10 hours in the refrigerator.
4. Then place the bowl containing dough at a warm place for a minimum of 15 hours.
5. After 15 hours, take a 9-by-5 inches bread pan, grease it with oil and set it aside until required.
6. Stir the dough, fold in cheese and chilies until evenly distributed, then shape the dough into round balls and place them into the prepared pan.
7. Brush the top of the dough with oil and then cover the pan with a greased plastic wrap.
8. Let the dough rest in a warm place for 2 hours and 30 minutes or more until the dough nears the plastic, then uncover the pan and let the dough rise until it reaches ½-inch above the rim of the pan.
9. When resting time is about to be over, switch on the oven, then set it to 425 degrees F (218°C) and let it preheat.
10. When ready to bake, switch the temperature of the oven to 400 degrees F (204°C) and then bake for 30 to 40 minutes or more until the crust turned golden brown.
11. Cover the top of the dough with foil and continue baking the bread for 20 to 30 minutes until the bread passes the toothpick test; a toothpick should come out clean from the pan or else continue baking for another 10 minutes.
12. When done, let the bread cool in its pan for 10 minutes, then carefully lift out the bread, and transfer it to a wire rack for 1 hour or more until cooled.
13. Cut bread into twelve slices and then serve.

Bacon Walnut Bread

This bread presents a wonderful combination of savory flavors of blue cheese dressing, bacon bits, and sweet honey flavor of butter.

Prep Time:	3 h 15 m	Calories:	296
Cook Time:	50 minutes	Fat (g):	23
Total Time:	4 h 5 m	Protein (g):	6
Servings:	16	Carbs:	17

Ingredients:

- All-purpose flour   2 cups
- Baking powder   2 teaspoons
- Baking soda   ½ teaspoon

- Yeast, active, dry   2 tablespoons
- Salt   ¼ teaspoon
- Ground black pepper   ¼ teaspoon
- Milk   1 cup
- Blue cheese salad dressing, refrigerated   ¾ cup
- Eggs, at room temperature   2
- Honey   1 tablespoon
- Chopped walnuts   2/3 cup
- Bacon bits   ½ cup

Instructions:

1. Take a large bowl, place flour in it, add salt, black pepper, yeast, baking powder, and soda and then stir until mixed.
2. Take a separate large bowl, crack the eggs in it, add remaining ingredients except for nuts and bacon, and whisk well until blended.
3. Whisk in flour mixture, ½ cup at a time, until incorporated and then fold in nuts and bacon until just mixed.
4. Cover the bowl with a plastic wrap and let it rest for a minimum of 3 hours at room temperature.
5. Spoon the dough onto a clean working space dusted with flour, knead it for 6 to 8 minutes until elastic.
6. Take a large piece of parchment sheet, use the dough scraper to flip the dough on the center of the sheet seam-side-down, and then gently shape the dough into a slightly oval shape. Cover it with the kitchen towel and let it rest for 1 hour.
7. Meanwhile, switch on the oven, set it to 375 degrees F (190°C), and let it preheat.
8. When ready to bake, use the parchment sheet to place the dough onto the sheet pan.
9. Bake for 50 minutes or more until the crust turned nicely brown and passes the toothpick test; a toothpick should come out clean from the pan or else continue baking for another 10 minutes.
10. When done, let the bread cool in its pan for 10 minutes, then carefully lift out the bread, and transfer it to a wire rack for 1 hour or more until cooled.
11. Cut bread into sixteen slices and then serve.

Irish Soda Bread

Any recipe for Irish soda bread is guaranteed to be a favorite of anyone who takes its bite.
Plus, you can adjust its recipes to your needs.

Prep Time:	15 minutes	Calories:	301
Cook Time:	50 minutes	Fat (g):	7
Total Time:	1h 5m	Protein (g):	8
Servings:	12	Carbs:	52

Ingredients:

- Butter, unsalted   4 tablespoons
- All-purpose flour   3 ½ cups

• Whole-wheat flour	½ cup
• Baking powder	2 teaspoons
• Baking soda	1 teaspoon
• Salt	1 teaspoon
• Buttermilk, chilled, divided	2 cups and 2 tablespoons
• Sugar	1 tablespoon
• Dried dill	1 tablespoon
• Lemon zest	1 tablespoon
• Raisins, soaked in water, drained	1 cup

Instructions:

1. Switch on the oven, place the baking rack in the middle section, then set it to 400 degrees F (204°C) and let it preheat.
2. Meanwhile, take an 8-inch skillet pan, grease it with oil and set it aside until required.
3. Cut the butter into small cubes, arrange them onto a plate and chill them in the refrigerator for 5 minutes.
4. Meanwhile, take a food processor or blender, add flours in it, and then add salt, sugar, dill, lemon zest, baking powder, and soda.
5. Add butter cubes and then pulse for 3 to 5 minutes until the mixture resembles crumbs.
6. Tip the mixture into a large bowl, stir 2 cups of buttermilk by using a wooden spoon until the dough comes together, fold in raisins and then shape the dough into an 8-inches round.
7. Flatten the dough, place it into the prepared skillet pan, then make a large 'X' across the dough, about ½-inch deep, and then brush the top with remaining buttermilk.
8. Transfer the skillet pan into the oven and then bake for 45 to 55 minutes or more until the crust turned golden brown and passes the toothpick test; a toothpick should come out clean from the pan or else continue baking for another 10 minutes.
9. When done, carefully lift out the bread and transfer it to a wire rack for 1 hour or more until cooled.
10. Cut bread into twelve slices and then serve.

Garlic Fontina Bread

Fontina cheese bread is a perfect family meal. It has a soft texture, and the crust is nicely brown. Enjoy it as a grilled sandwich or use it for garlic bread toast.

Prep Time:	1 h 45 m	Calories:	119
Cook Time:	35 minutes	Fat (g):	4
Total Time:	2 h 20 m	Protein (g):	4
Servings:	16	Carbs:	17

Ingredients:

- Yeast, active, dry   ¼ oz (7 g)
- Water, at 110 degrees F   1 cup
- Sugar   1 ½ tablespoons
- Vegetable shortening   1 tablespoon
- Garlic powder   ½ tablespoon
- Salt   1 teaspoon
- All-purpose flour   2 ½ cups
- Fontina cheese, shredded, divided   ¾ cup and 1 tablespoon
- Olive oil   ¾ tablespoon

Instructions:

1. Take a large bowl, place yeast in it, stir in water until combined, and then beat in garlic powder, salt, shortening, sugar, and flour, ½ cup at a time, until incorporated.
2. Fold in ¾ cup of cheese, then spoon the dough onto a clean working space dusted with flour and knead it for 8 minutes until elastic.
3. Take a large bowl, grease it with oil, place the dough in it, brush the top with oil, cover the bowl with a kitchen towel and let it rest for a minimum of 1 hour at a warm place until doubled in size.
4. Meanwhile, take a 9-by-5 inches bread pan, grease it with oil and set it aside until required.
5. Then punch down the dough, shape it into a round, place it into the prepared pan, cover it with a plastic wrap and let it rest for a minimum of 30 minutes at a warm place until raised.
6. Meanwhile, switch on the oven, then set it to 375 degrees F (190°C) and let it preheat.
7. Then uncover the bread pan, brush the top of the dough with oil, sprinkle with remaining cheese and then bake for 30 to 35 minutes or more until the crust turned nicely brown and passes the toothpick test; a toothpick should come out clean from the pan or else continue baking for another 10 minutes.
8. When done, let the bread cool in its pan for 10 minutes, then carefully lift out the bread, and transfer it to a wire rack for 1 hour or more until cooled.
9. Cut bread into sixteen slices and then serve.

Lemon Yogurt Bread

This tender sweet loaf will remind you of a pound cake. Its cake-like texture and lemon flavor make it perfect for an afternoon snack, brunch, or dessert.

Prep Time:	15 minutes	Calories:	177
Cook Time:	50 minutes	Fat (g):	7
Total Time:	1 h 5 m	Protein (g):	3
Servings:	12	Carbs:	26

Ingredients:

- All-purpose flour   1 ½ cups
- Sugar   ¾ cup
- Salt   ½ teaspoon
- Baking soda   ½ teaspoon
- Baking powder   ¼ teaspoon
- Egg, at room temperature   1
- Lemon yogurt   1 cup
- Olive oil   1/3 cup
- Lemon juice   1 tablespoon

Instructions:

1. Switch on the oven, then set it to 325 degrees F (163°C) and let it preheat.
2. Meanwhile, take an 8-by-4 inches bread pan, grease it with oil and set it aside until required.
3. Take a large bowl, place flour in it, add salt, sugar, baking powder, and soda and then stir until mixed.
4. Take a separate large bowl, crack the egg in it, pour in oil, lemon juice, and yogurt, and then whisk until combined.
5. Beat flour mixture into the egg mixture, ½ cup at a time, until incorporated and then pour the mixture into the prepared pan.
6. Bake for 45 to 50 minutes or more until the crust turned golden brown and passes the toothpick test; a toothpick should come out clean from the pan or else continue baking for another 10 minutes.
7. When done, let the bread cool in its pan for 10 minutes, then carefully lift out the bread, and transfer it to a wire rack for 1 hour or more until cooled.
8. Cut bread into twelve slices and then serve.

Skillet Herb Bread

It offers a perfect balance between crumbly and tender texture.

Prep Time:	15 minutes	Calories:	275
Cook Time:	45 minutes	Fat (g):	9
Total Time:	1h	Protein (g):	7
Servings:	10	Carbs:	40

Ingredients:

• All-purpose flour	1 ½ cups
• Sugar	2 tablespoons
• Baking powder	4 teaspoons
• Salt	1 ½ teaspoons
• Dried sage	1 teaspoon
• Dried thyme	1 teaspoon
• Cornmeal	1 ½ cups
• Celery, chopped	1 ½ cups
• White onion, peeled, chopped	1 cup
• Pimientos, chopped	2 oz (57 g)
• Egg, at room temperature	3
• Milk	1 ½ cups
• Olive oil	1/3 cup

Instructions:

1. Switch on the oven, then set it to 400 degrees F (204°C) and let it preheat.
2. Meanwhile, take a 10 inches skillet pan, grease it with oil and set it aside until required.
3. Take a large bowl, place flour in it, add salt, sugar, sage, thyme, and baking powder and stir until combined.
4. Take a medium bowl, place cornmeal in it, stir in pimientos, onion, and celery, add the mixture into the flour mixture and then stir until well combined.
5. Take a separate medium bowl, crack eggs in it, whisk in oil and milk until blended, and beat this mixture into the flour mixture until smooth.
6. Spoon the batter into the prepared skillet and then bake for 35 to 45 minutes or more until the crust turned golden brown and passes the toothpick test; a toothpick should come out clean from the pan or else continue baking for another 10 minutes.
7. When done, carefully lift out the bread and transfer it to a wire rack for 30 minutes or more until cooled.
8. Cut bread into ten slices and then serve.

French Baguettes

If you are looking for something to compliment chowder, salad, or pasta meals, then try French baguettes. You won't be able to stop eating them when it will come out of the oven.

Prep Time:	1h 30 m	Calories:	881
Cook Time:	25 minutes	Fat (g):	8
Total Time:	1 h 55 m	Protein (g):	35
Servings:	2	Carbs:	168

Ingredients:

• All-purpose flour	2 ½ cups
• Sugar	1 tablespoon
• Yeast, active, dry	1 ½ teaspoons
• Water, warm	1 cup
• Salt	1 teaspoon

Instructions:

1. Take a large bowl, place flour in it, add yeast and sugar, pour in warm water, and then beat by using an electric mixer until dough comes together.
2. Cover the bowl with a kitchen towel or plastic wrap and let it rest for 15 minutes at a warm place.
3. Knead salt into the dough, cover the bowl again with a kitchen towel and let it rest at a warm place for 30 minutes until doubled in size.
4. Then spoon the dough onto a clean working space dusted with flour, roll it into a 16-by-12 inches rectangle and then cut it into two pieces, each about an 8-by-12 inch rectangle.
5. Working on one dough at a time, roll it tightly, starting from the 12-inch side, flatten out the air bubbles and then taper off the ends.
6. Transfer the loaf onto a baking sheet greased with oil and then repeat with the remaining dough.
7. When done, make a few slashes on the top of each loaf, cover them with a kitchen towel and let the loaves rest for a minimum of 40 minutes at a warm place until doubled in size.
8. Meanwhile, switch on the oven, then set it to 375 degrees F (190°C) and let it preheat.
9. Bake the loaves for 25 minutes or more until the crust turned golden brown and the loaves pass the toothpick test; a toothpick should come out clean from the pan or else continue baking for another 10 minutes.
10. When done, let the bread cool in the baking sheet for 10 minutes and then serve.

Sun-Dried Tomato Provolone Bread

This savory bread is packed with great flavors. It makes a scrumptious accompaniment with meat dishes and also goes great with chowders and soups.

Prep Time:	15 minutes	Calories:	121
Cook Time:	50 minutes	Fat (g):	5
Total Time:	1h 5 m	Protein (g):	5
Servings:	6	Carbs:	14

Ingredients:

- Sun-dried tomatoes, oil-packed, drained, chopped   1/3 cup
- All-purpose flour   2 ¼ cups

- Baking powder ..... 2 teaspoons
- Sugar ..... 2 teaspoons
- Dried basil ..... 1 ¼ teaspoons
- Salt ..... 1 teaspoon
- Baking soda ..... ½ teaspoon
- Ground black pepper ..... ½ teaspoon
- Eggs, at room temperature 2
- Buttermilk ..... 1 ¼ cups
- Olive oil ..... 3 tablespoons
- Oil from sun-dried tomatoes ..... 2 tablespoons
- Provolone cheese, shredded ..... 1 cup
- Parsley, minced ..... ¼ cup
- Italian seasoning ..... ½ teaspoon

Instructions:

1. Switch on the oven, then set it to 350 degrees F (177°C) and let it preheat.
2. Meanwhile, take an 8-by-4 inches bread pan, grease it with oil and set it aside until required.
3. Take a large bowl, place flour in it, add salt, sugar, basil, black pepper, baking powder, and soda and then stir until combined.
4. Take a medium bowl, crack eggs in it, pour in olive oil, sun-dried tomato oil, and buttermilk and then whisk until blended.
5. Pour the egg mixture into the mixture of flour, beat until incorporated, and then fold in the tomatoes, cheese, and parsley until just mixed.
6. Transfer the mixture into the prepared pan, sprinkle the seasoning on top and then bake for 40 to 50 minutes or more until the crust turned golden brown and passes the toothpick test; a toothpick should come out clean from the pan or else continue baking for another 10 minutes.
7. When done, let the loaves cool in its pan for 10 minutes, then carefully lift out the bread, and transfer it to a wire rack for 30 minutes or more until cooled.
8. Serve straight away.

Bagels

These bagels are much better than the store-bought ones and also way cheaper.

Prep Time:	2 h 30 m	Calories:	270
Cook Time:	50 minutes	Fat (g):	2
Total Time:	3 h 20 m	Protein (g):	10
Servings:	8	Carbs:	53

Ingredients:

- Water, at 110 degrees F   1 ½ cups
- Yeast, active, dry   1 tablespoon
- Brown sugar   1 tablespoon
- All-purpose flour   4 cups

- Salt   2 teaspoons
- Water, at room temperature   8 cups
- Cane sugar   1 tablespoon
- White sesame seeds   3 teaspoons

Instructions:

1. Take a large bowl, pour in warm water, sprinkle with yeast and brown sugar, stir well and then let the mixture rest for 5 minutes until emulsified.
2. Whisk in salt and flour by using an electric beater until incorporated, then spoon the dough onto a clean working space dusted with flour and knead for 10 minutes until elastic.
3. Take a large bowl, grease it with oil, place dough in it, brush oil on top, then cover the bowl with a kitchen towel and let it rest for a minimum of 1 hour and 30 minutes at a warm place.
4. Then spoon the dough onto a clean working space dusted with flour, divide it evenly into eight pieces and then shape each piece into a round ball.
5. Cover the balls with a kitchen towel and then let them rest for a minimum for 30 minutes at a warm place.
6. Meanwhile, prepare the water bath for bagels and for this, take a large pot, place it over medium heat, pour in water and cane sugar, and bring it to a gentle simmer.
7. Switch on the oven, then set it to 425 degrees F (218°C) and let it preheat.
8. After 30 minutes, prepare bagel and for this, take a dough ball, poke a hole in its center and then stretch the hole about 2-inch by using the finger.
9. Place prepared bagel onto a baking sheet greased with oil and then prepare more bagels from the remaining dough balls in the same manner.
10. Then carefully drop bagels into simmering water, don't crowd the pot, and switch heat to medium-high level to bring water to a gentle boil.
11. Simmer bagels for 2 minutes, flip them, continue simmering for 1 minute and then return them onto the baking sheet by using a strainer.
12. Repeat with the remaining bagels, bake them for 15 minutes, then sprinkle seeds on top of bagels and continue baking for 10 minutes until golden brown.
13. When done, transfer bagels onto the wire rack and cool them for 10 minutes.
14. Serve straight away.

Seeded Savory Bread

This delicious savory bread is packed with whole grains, sunflower seeds, sesame seeds, and flaxseeds. All you need is to mix these ingredients and pop the dough into the oven.

Prep Time:	15 minutes	Calories:	99
Cook Time:	1h 5 m	Fat (g):	2
Total Time:	1 h 20 m	Protein (g):	6
Servings:	12	Carbs:	15

Ingredients:

- Honey   1 tablespoons
- Olive oil   2 tablespoons
- Whole-wheat flour   2 cups

- Spelt flour — 2 cups
- Sunflower seeds, toasted — ½ cup and 2 teaspoons
- Black sesame seeds — ½ cup and 1 teaspoon
- Caraway seeds — 2 tablespoons and 1 teaspoon
- Oats, old-fashion — 1 teaspoon
- Flaxseeds — 2 tablespoons and 1 teaspoon
- Baking powder — 2 teaspoons
- Baking soda — 1 teaspoon
- Salt — 2 teaspoons
- Whole milk, at room temperature — 1 ½ cups
- Buttermilk, at room temperature — ¾ cup

Instructions:

1. Switch on the oven, then set it to 350 degrees F (177°C) and let it preheat.
2. Meanwhile, take a 9-by-5 inches bread pan, grease it with oil, then line it with parchment paper and set it aside until required.
3. Take a large bowl, place flour in it, add salt, baking powder, baking soda, ½ cup each of black sesame seeds and sunflower seeds, 2 tablespoons of flaxseeds and caraway seeds, and then stir until mixed.
4. Take a separate large bowl, pour in the whole milk and buttermilk, oil, and honey, and then whisk until the honey has dissolved completely.
5. Beat in flour mixture, ½ cup at a time, until incorporated, transfer the mixture into the prepared pan and then sprinkle remaining seeds on top.
6. Bake the bread for 1 hour and 5 minutes or more until the crust turned nicely brown and passes the toothpick test; a toothpick should come out clean from the pan or else continue baking for another 10 minutes.
7. When done, let the bread cool in its pan for 15 minutes, then carefully lift out the bread, and transfer it to a wire rack for 1 hour or more until cooled.
8. Cut bread into twelve slices and then serve.

Round Cheese Bread

Prep Time:	15 minutes	Calories:	183
Cook Time:	25 minutes	Fat (g):	10
Total Time:	40 minutes	Protein (g):	7
Servings:	8	Carbs:	15

Ingredients:

•	Baking mix	1 ½ cups
•	Mozzarella cheese, shredded	1 cup
•	Parmesan cheese, grated	¼ cup and more as needed
•	Dried oregano	½ teaspoon
•	Milk, at room temperature	½ cup
•	Egg, at room temperature	1
•	Butter, unsalted, melted	2 tablespoons

Instructions:

1. Switch on the oven, then set it to 400 degrees F (204°C) and let it preheat.
2. Meanwhile, take a 9 inches round baking pan, grease it with oil, and set it aside until required.
3. Take a large bowl, place flour in it, add remaining ingredients in it except for butter and then whisk well by using an electric beater until incorporated and smooth batter comes together.
4. Transfer the mixture into the prepared pan, drizzle butter on top, sprinkle with some more parmesan cheese, and then bake for 20 to 25 minutes or more until the crust turned nicely brown and passes the toothpick test; a toothpick should come out clean from the pan or else continue baking for another 10 minutes.
5. When done, let the bread cool in its pan for 10 minutes, cut bread into eight slices and then serve.

Spicy Cheese Bread

It needs only five ingredients to come together and need only 30 minutes of your time, from start to finish.

Prep Time:	15 minutes	Calories:	207
Cook Time:	15 minutes	Fat (g):	8
Total Time:	30 minutes	Protein (g):	6
Servings:	8	Carbs:	27

Ingredients:

- Ground black pepper   ¾ teaspoon
- Butter, unsalted   2 tablespoons
- Olive oil   1 tablespoon
- Pizza crust, refrigerated   13.8 oz (391 g)
- Parmesan cheese, grated   ¼ cup

Instructions:

1. Switch on the oven, then set it to 450 degrees F (232°C) and let it preheat.
2. Meanwhile, take a 9 inches skillet pan; brush it with the olive oil, unroll the pizza crust in it, flatten it and spread it along the edges, and then top the dough with butter, cheese, and black pepper.
3. Bake for 10 to 15 minutes or more until the crust turned golden brown, and when done, let the bread cool in its pan for 10 minutes.
4. Cut bread into eight slices and then serve.

Whole-Grain Artisan Bread

This artisan bread is loaded with whole-grains and required no kneading and proofing.
The dough can also be stored in the refrigerator for up to 14 days.

Prep Time:	3 h 40 m	Calories:	60
Cook Time:	30 minutes	Fat (g):	1
Total Time:	4 h 10 m	Protein (g):	3
Servings:	12	Carbs:	11

Ingredients:

- Whole-wheat flour   1 1/3 cups
- All-purpose flour   ½ cup
- Yeast, active, dry   1/3 tablespoon

- Salt   ¼ tablespoon
- Wheat gluten   1 tablespoon
- Water, at 100 degrees F   1 cup
- White sesame seeds   1 teaspoon
- Flaxseeds   1 teaspoon
- Pumpkin seeds   1 teaspoon
- Sunflower seeds   1 teaspoon

Instructions:

1. Take a large bowl, place both flours in it, add salt, yeast, and wheat gluten in it and then stir until mixed.
2. Whisk in water by using an electric beater until moist mixture comes together, cover the bowl with a plastic wrap and let it rest for a minimum of 2 hours or 8 hours at room temperature until the top of the dough flattens.
3. Meanwhile, take a baking sheet, line it with parchment paper, and dust it with flour.
4. Transfer dough onto the prepared baking sheet, shape it into a smooth round-shape ball by using floured hands, and then let it rest for 1 hour and 30 minutes at room temperature.
5. Meanwhile, switch on the oven, set it to 450 degrees F (232°C), then place a Dutch oven in it and let it preheat.
6. When ready to bake, sprinkle all the seeds on top of the dough, make some ¼-inch deep cuts across the top and then carefully spoon the dough along with the parchment paper into the heated Dutch oven.
7. Return Dutch oven into the oven, cover it with lid, bake for 20 minutes, then uncover it and continue baking for 10 minutes until the crust turned golden brown and passes the toothpick test; a toothpick should come out clean from the pan or else continue baking for another 10 minutes.
8. When done, let the bread cool in its pan for 10 minutes, then carefully lift out the bread by using parchment paper, and transfer it to a wire rack for 1 hour or more until cooled.
9. Cut bread into twelve slices and then serve.

Sour Cream and Banana Bread

The sour cream in the recipe makes the loaf so moist that it melts in the mouth. Plus, it has wonderful flavors. Make some extra loaves and freeze them for later.

Prep Time:	15 minutes	Calories:	263
Cook Time:	60 minutes	Fat (g):	10
Total Time:	1 h 15 m	Protein (g):	4
Servings:	8	Carbs:	40

Ingredients:

• All-purpose flour	1 cup
• Sugar	¾ cups + 1 tablespoon
• Ground cinnamon	½ teaspoon
• Butter, unsalted	3 tablespoons
• Egg, at room temperature	1
• Banana, peeled, mashed	1 ½
• Sour cream	4 oz (113 g)
• Vanilla extract	½ teaspoon
• Salt	1/8 teaspoon
• Baking soda	¾ teaspoon
• Walnuts, chopped	1/3 cup

Instructions:

1. Switch on the oven, then set it to 300 degrees F (149°C) and let it preheat.
2. Meanwhile, take a small bowl, place 1 tablespoon of sugar in it, stir in ¼ teaspoon of cinnamon and then sprinkle this mixture into a 9-by-5 inches bread pan, set it aside until required.
3. Take a large bowl, place butter in it, and then whisk in the remaining sugar until creamy and then whisk in bananas, the remaining cinnamon, vanilla, sour cream, and egg by using an electric beater until combined.
4. Whisk in baking soda, salt, and flour, ½ cup at a time, until incorporated and then fold in walnuts until just mixed.
5. Spoon the mixture into the prepared bread pan and then bake for 60 minutes or more until the crust turned golden brown and passes the toothpick test; a toothpick should come out clean from the pan or else continue baking for another 10 minutes.
6. When done, let the bread cool in its pan for 10 minutes, then carefully lift out the bread, and transfer it to a wire rack for 1 hour or more until cooled.
7. Cut bread into eight slices and then serve.

Savory Cheese Bread

It will only take one hour, from start to finish.

Prep Time:	15 minutes	Calories:	240
Cook Time:	40 minutes	Fat (g):	10
Total Time:	55 minutes	Protein (g):	10
Servings:	12	Carbs:	28

Ingredients:

- All-purpose flour   3 cups
- Baking powder   2 teaspoons

- Salt   1 ¼ teaspoons
- Parmesan cheese, grated   1 cup
- Mozzarella cheese, shredded   1 cup
- Butter, unsalted, softened   ¼ cup
- Eggs, at room temperature   4
- Whole milk, at room temperature   ½ cup
- Minced garlic   1 tablespoon
- Sun-dried tomatoes, oil-packed, drained, chopped   ½ cup

Instructions:

1. Switch on the oven, then set it to 350 degrees F (177°C) and let it preheat.
2. Meanwhile, take a baking sheet, grease it with oil, and set it aside until required.
3. Take a large bowl, place flour in it, add salt, baking powder, butter, and cheeses and then whisk well by using an electric beater until mixture resembles crumbs.
4. Add tomatoes, garlic into the flour mixture, and then stir until mixed.
5. Take a separate large bowl, crack eggs in it, whisk in milk until blended, and then whisk in flour mixture, ½ cup at a time, until smooth batter comes together.
6. Spoon the dough onto a clean working space dusted with flour, knead it for 6 to 8 minutes until elastic and then shape it into a round loaf.
7. Transfer the dough onto the prepared sheet pan, and then bake for 40 minutes or more until the crust turned golden brown and passes the toothpick test; a toothpick should come out clean from the pan or else continue baking for another 10 minutes.
8. When done, let the bread cool in its pan for 10 minutes, then carefully lift out the bread and transfer it to a wire rack for 20 minutes.
9. Cut bread into twelve slices and then serve.

Irish Soda Bread with Cheese

Take your regular Irish soda bread to another level by incorporating cheese and herbs. It comes together within an hour and goes great with salads and soups.

Prep Time:	15 minutes	Calories:	168
Cook Time:	30 minutes	Fat (g):	6
Total Time:	45 minutes	Protein (g):	7
Servings:	10	Carbs:	21

Ingredients:

• All-purpose flour	2 cups
• Baking soda	½ teaspoon
• Baking powder	1 teaspoon
• Salt	½ teaspoon
• Cheddar cheese, grated	4 oz (113 g)
• Buttermilk	1 cup
• Egg, at room temperature	1

Instructions:

1. Switch on the oven, then set it to 425 degrees F (218°C) and let it preheat.
2. Meanwhile, take a large sheet pan, line it with parchment paper, dust it with flour and set it aside until required.
3. Take a large bowl, place flour in it, add salt, baking powder, and soda, stir until combined, and then stir in cheese until just mixture resembles crumbs.
4. Take a small bowl, crack the egg in it, whisk in buttermilk, and then whisk this mixture into the flour mixture by using an immersion blender until incorporated.
5. Spoon the dough onto a clean working space dusted with flour, knead it for 6 to 8 minutes until elastic and then shape it into a round loaf.
6. Spoon the dough onto the prepared sheet pan, make a big 'X' across the top by using a sharp knife and then bake for 30 minutes or more until the crust turned nicely brown and passes the toothpick test; a toothpick should come out clean from the pan or else continue baking for another 10 minutes.
7. When done, let the bread cool in the sheet pan for 20 minutes.
8. Cut bread into ten slices and then serve.

Bacon and Cheese Bread

Bake this moist, soft and delicious bread with bacon bits and cheddar cheese. It is excellent for breakfast, brunch, or snack.

Prep Time:	20 minutes	Calories:	341
Cook Time:	50 minutes	Fat (g):	18
Total Time:	1 h 10 m	Protein (g):	12
Servings:	10	Carbs:	33

Ingredients:

- All-purpose flour   1 ¼ cups
- Bread flour   1 cup

- Baking powder   2 teaspoons
- Baking soda   ½ teaspoon
- Salt   1 teaspoon
- Cheddar cheese, cubed   4 oz (113 g)
- Cheddar cheese, grated   2 oz (57 g)
- Bacon strips, cooked, chopped   10
- Eggs, at room temperature   2
- Olive oil   2 ½ tablespoons
- Buttermilk   1 ¼ cups

Instructions:

1. Switch on the oven, then set it to 350 degrees F (177°C) and let it preheat.
2. Meanwhile, take an 8-by-4 inches bread pan, grease it with oil and set it aside until required.
3. Take a large bowl, place both flours in it, add salt, baking powder, and soda, stir until mixed and stir in cheese (cubed), and chopped bacon strips until combined.
4. Take a medium bowl, crack eggs in it, beat in oil and buttermilk by using an electric beater until blended, and then whisk this mixture into the flour mixture by using a wooden spoon until incorporated and smooth batter for dough comes together.
5. Spoon the dough into the prepared pan, spread it evenly, spread the remaining cheddar cheese (grated), and then bake for 50 minutes or more until the crust turned golden brown and passes the toothpick test; a toothpick should come out clean from the pan or else continue baking for another 10 minutes.
6. When done, let the bread cool in its pan for 10 minutes, then carefully lift out the bread, and cut it into ten slices.
7. Serve straight away.

Honey French Bread

Combine savory and sweet flavors in one loaf, which is satisfying and tasty. It will please everyone at your dinner table.

Prep Time:	2 h 25 m	Calories:	124
Cook Time:	40 minutes	Fat (g):	0
Total Time:	3 h 5 m	Protein (g):	4
Servings:	10	Carbs:	27

Ingredients:

- Yeast, active, dry   ½ tablespoon
- All-purpose flour   2 ½ cups
- Water, lukewarm   1 cup
- Salt   ½ teaspoon
- Honey   ½ tablespoon

Instructions:

1. Take a large bowl, place flour in it, add remaining ingredients and then whisk by using an immersion blender until incorporated and smooth batter for dough comes together.

2. Let the mixture rest at room temperature for 15 minutes, then spoon the dough onto a clean working space dusted with flour and then knead it 5 minutes until elastic.

3. Take a large bowl, grease it with oil, place dough in it, brush the top with oil, cover the bowl with a kitchen towel and let it rest for 1 hour at warm temperature until doubled in size.

4. Then take a baking sheet and line it with parchment paper.

5. When the dough has raised, lunch it down, transfer to the prepared baking sheet, shape it into a roll, cover it with a kitchen towel and let it rise for another hour at the room temperature.

6. When the resting time is about to over, switch on the oven, then set it to 400 degrees F (204°C) and let it preheat.

7. When the dough is ready for baking, make three cuts on its top by using a sharp knife.

8. Bake for 30 to 40 minutes or more until the crust turned golden brown and passes the toothpick test; a toothpick should come out clean from the pan or else continue baking for another 10 minutes.

9. When done, let the bread cool in its pan for 10 minutes, then carefully lift out the bread, and transfer it to a wire rack for 1 hour or more until cooled.

10. Cut bread into 8 slices and then serve.

Honey Whole-Wheat Bread

This loaf is the best sandwich bread and much better than the commercial brands. You will feel good by feeding this bread to your family. And, you will be surprised how easy it is to prep and bake it.

Prep Time:	1 h 20 m	Calories:	108
Cook Time:	25 minutes	Fat (g):	1
Total Time:	1 h 45 m	Protein (g):	3
Servings:	16	Carbs:	19

Ingredients:

- Whole-wheat flour   1 cup
- Bread flour   2 cups
- Sugar   1 tablespoon

- Salt   ¾ teaspoon
- Yeast, active, dry   ¼ oz (7 g)
- Honey   2 tablespoons
- Water, at 110 degrees F   ¾ cup
- Milk   1/3 cup
- Butter, unsalted, softened   3 tablespoons

Instructions:

1. Take a large bowl, place both flours in it, add yeast, salt, and sugar, and then stir until mixed.
2. Take a medium bowl, add honey and butter in it, pour in water and milk, and whisk well until blended.
3. Pour milk mixture into the flour mixture, whisk well by using an immersion blender until incorporated and smooth batter for dough comes together.
4. Transfer dough onto a clean working space dusted with flour, knead it for 5 minutes until elastic and then shape it into a round.
5. Take a large bowl, grease it with oil, place dough in it, brush the top with oil, cover the bowl with a kitchen towel and let it rest for 30 minutes or more at warm temperature until doubled in size.
6. Then spoon the dough onto a clean working space dusted with flour, roll it into a 10-by-12 inch rectangle, then roll it like a cigar and pinch the seams.
7. Roll the dough more to shape it like a uniform log and then place it onto a 9-by-5 inches bread pan seam-side-down.
8. Brush the dough with oil, cover with a kitchen towel and let it rest for 30 minutes or more at a warm place until the dough rises 1-inch above the top of the pan.
9. Meanwhile, switch on the oven, then set it to 400 degrees F (204°C) and let it preheat.
10. Bake for 25 minutes or more until the crust turned golden brown and passes the toothpick test; a toothpick should come out clean from the pan or else continue baking for another 10 minutes.
11. When done, let the bread cool in its pan for 10 minutes, then carefully lift out the bread, and transfer it to a wire rack for 1 hour or more until cooled.
12. Cut bread into sixteen slices and then serve.

Apple Pie Stuffed Monkey Bread

Celebrate this fall with this amazing monkey bread. Get it stuffed with apples and elevate its flavors with cinnamon and apple pie spice. You can give it as a gift to your friends and family.

Prep Time:	2 h 20 m	Calories:	114
Cook Time:	30 minutes	Fat (g):	6
Total Time:	2 h 50 m	Protein (g):	2
Servings:	16	Carbs:	12

Ingredients:

For the Bread:

- Milk, at 104 degrees F   ½ cup
- Yeast, active, dry   ¼ oz (7 g)
- Sugar   ¼ cup
- Salt   ½ teaspoon
- Egg   1
- Butter, unsalted, melted   2 tablespoons

- Diced apple chunks   1 can (20 oz; 567 g)
- Apple pie spice   1 teaspoon
- Bread flour   3 cups

  For the Coating:
- Sugar   ½ cup
- Apple pie spice   1 teaspoon

Instructions:

1. Take a large bowl, pour in milk, stir in sugar, then sprinkle with yeast and let it stand for 5 minutes.
2. Then add egg, salt, apple pie spice, and butter, whisk well by using an electric beater until mixed and then beat in flour, ½ cup at a time until incorporated and smooth batter for dough comes together.
3. Spoon the dough onto a clean working space dusted with flour, knead it for 5 minutes and then shape it into a round.
4. Take a large bowl, grease it with oil, place dough in it, brush the top with oil, cover the bowl with a kitchen towel and let it rest for 1 hour or more at warm temperature until doubled in size.
5. Meanwhile, take a Bundt pan, grease it with oil and set it aside until required.
6. Prepare coating for the bread, and for this, take a small bowl, add sugar and apple pie spice in it and then stir until mixed, set aside until required.
7. When the dough has risen, take a small portion of it, about egg-size, spread it into a small disk, place ½ teaspoon of apple chunks, pinch together the edges, roll it into a ball and then coat with coating mixture and place into the prepared pan.
8. Repeat with the remaining dough, arrange into the Bundt pan, and when done, cover lightly with a plastic wrap and let it stand for 1 hour at a warm place.
9. Meanwhile, switch on the oven, then set it to 350 degrees F (177°C) and let it preheat.
10. Uncover the Bundt pan, place it into the oven and then bake for 30 minutes or more until the crust turned golden brown.
11. When done, let the bread cool in its pan for 30 minutes, and then invert the pan over a pan to take out the bread.
12. Serve straight away.

Chocolate Banana Bread

Prep Time:	15 minutes	Calories:	293
Cook Time:	60 minutes	Fat (g):	15
Total Time:	1 h 15 m	Protein (g):	3
Servings:	12	Carbs:	41

Ingredients:

• Butter, unsalted, softened	½ cup
• Sugar	1 cup
• Eggs, at room temperature	2
• Bananas	1 cup
• Milk, at room temperature	¼ cup
• Vanilla extract, unsweetened	1 teaspoon
• All-purpose flour	2 cups
• Cocoa powder, unsweetened	¼ cup
• Baking soda	1 teaspoon
• Salt	1 teaspoon
• Mini chocolate chips	¼ cup

Instructions:

1. Switch on the oven, then set it to 350 degrees F (177°C) and let it preheat.
2. Meanwhile, take a 9-by-5 inches bread pan, grease it with oil and set it aside until required.
3. Take a large bowl, place butter in it, beat in sugar until fluffy, and then beat in bananas, eggs, vanilla, and milk until blended.
4. Take a separate large bowl, place flour in it, add salt, baking soda, and cocoa powder and stir until mixed.
5. Stir flour mixture into the banana mixture until incorporated, don't over-mix, and then pour the mixture into the prepared pan.
6. Spread the mixture evenly and bake for 1 hour or more until the bread passes the toothpick test; a toothpick should come out clean from the pan or else continue baking for another 10 minutes.
7. When done, top with chocolate chips and let the bread cool in its pan for 10 minutes, then carefully lift out the bread, and transfer it to a wire rack for 1 hour or more until cooled.
8. Cut bread into twelve slices and then serve.

Cranberry Bread

If you are hosting a tea party or a family brunch, then this cranberry bread is perfect for impressing your guests. The cranberries add natural sweetness to the loaf, lemon zest add brightens every bite, while pecans add crunchiness and improve texture.

Prep Time:	20 minutes	Calories:	218
Cook Time:	1 h 10 m	Fat (g):	3
Total Time:	1 h 30 m	Protein (g):	4
Servings:	8	Carbs:	44

Ingredients:

- Vegetable shortening   ½ cup
- Pecans, chopped   1 ½ cups

- Cranberries, halves, fresh or frozen   1 ½ cups
- Sugar   1 ¼ cups
- All-purpose flour   3 cups
- Baking powder   4 ½ teaspoons
- Salt   ½ teaspoon
- Lemon zest   2 teaspoons
- Eggs, at room temperature   2
- Milk, at room temperature   1 cup

Instructions:

1. Switch on the oven, then set it to 350 degrees F (177°C) and let it preheat.
2. Meanwhile, take a Bundt pan, grease it with oil, sprinkle ½ cup pecans in its bottom, and then set it aside until required.
3. Take a medium bowl, place berries in it, stir in ¼ cup of sugar and let it stand until required.
4. Place flour in a food processor, add remaining sugar, salt, baking powder, and pulse the mixture for 3 minutes until it resembles crumbs. Cut in shortening with a pastry blender. Mix well.
5. Tip the mixture into a large bowl, add lemon zest and remaining pecans, and then stir until mixed.
6. Take a small bowl, crack eggs in it and then beat in milk until blended.
7. Pour egg mixture into the mixture of flour, stir well by using a wooden spoon until incorporated and the dough comes together and then fold in cranberries.
8. Spoon the dough into the prepared Bundt pan and then bake for 1 hour and 10 minutes or more until the crust turned golden brown and passes the toothpick test; a toothpick should come out clean from the pan or else continue baking for another 10 minutes.
9. When done, let the bread cool in its pan for 10 minutes, then carefully lift out the bread, and transfer it to a wire rack for 1 hour or more until cooled.
10. Cut bread into eight slices and then serve.

Dried Fruit and Cinnamon Bread

This sweet bread will become a show-stopper for your next dessert.

Prep Time:	1 h 15 m	Calories:	170
Cook Time:	45 minutes	Fat (g):	3
Total Time:	2 hours	Protein (g):	3
Servings:	12	Carbs:	31

Ingredients:

<u>For the Bread</u>:

- All-purpose flour   3 cups
- Sugar   ¼ cup
- Salt   1 teaspoon
- Ground cinnamon   2 teaspoons

- Yeast, active, dry   2 ¼ teaspoons
- Butter, melted   ¼ cup
- Water, at 130 degrees F   1 ¼ cups
- Egg, at room temperature   1
- Dried fruit mixture, diced   1 cup

  For the Glaze:
- Powdered sugar   ½ cup
- Vanilla extract, unsweetened   ¼ teaspoon
- Milk   3 teaspoons

Instructions:

1. Meanwhile, take a 9-by-5 inches bread pan, grease it with oil and set it aside until required.
2. Take a large bowl, place 2 cups flour in it, add salt, cinnamon, yeast, and sugar in it and then stir until mixed.
3. Take a medium bowl, crack the egg in it and then beat in butter and water until blended.
4. Pour the egg mixture into the mixture of flour, beat until incorporated, and then stir in remaining flour and dried fruit mixture until just mixed.
5. Spoon the dough into the prepared pan, spread it evenly, cover with lightly with greased plastic wrap and then let it rest for 1 hour at a warm place until doubled in size.
6. Meanwhile, switch on the oven, then set it to 375 degrees F (190°C) and let it pre-heat.
7. Bake for 45 minutes or more until the crust turned golden brown and passes the toothpick test; a toothpick should come out clean from the pan or else continue baking for another 10 minutes.
8. When done, carefully lift out the bread from the pan and transfer it to a wire rack for 1 hour or more until cooled.
9. Meanwhile, prepare the glaze and for this, take a medium bowl, place all of its ingredients in it and then whisk until smooth.
10. Drizzle the glaze over the bread, cut it into twelve slices, and then serve.

Pumpkin Bread with Cream Cheese Filling

This sweetened bread is loaded with cream cheese, which elevates the moistness of this bread. Make an extra loaf, cut it into slices, freeze it for later, and then take it out when you need a snack. It is also perfect as a gift for a Thanksgiving dinner.

Prep Time:	20 minutes	Calories:	237
Cook Time:	1 h 10 minutes	Fat (g):	14
Total Time:	1 h 30 m	Protein (g):	5
Servings:	12	Carbs:	24

Ingredients:

For the Bread:

• All-purpose flour	¾ cup and 1 tablespoon
• Baking soda	½ teaspoon
• Salt	¼ teaspoon
• Ground cinnamon	½ teaspoon

- Ginger powder   1/8 teaspoon
- Nutmeg, ground   1/8 teaspoon
- Pumpkin puree   ½ cup
- Olive oil   ¼ cup
- Eggs, at room temperature   1
- Sugar   ¾ cup

  For the Filling:
- Cream cheese, softened   4 oz (113 g)
- Sugar   ¼ cup
- All-purpose flour   ½ tablespoon
- Egg, at room temperature   ½

Instructions:

1. Switch on the oven, then set it to 325 degrees F (163°C) and let it preheat.
2. Meanwhile, take an 8-by-4 inches bread pan, grease it with oil and set it aside until required.
3. Prepare the filling and for this, take a medium bowl, place all of its ingredients in it, whisk well by using an electric beater until blended, and then set aside until required.
4. Prepare the bread and for this, take a large bowl, place flour in it, add salt, ginger, nutmeg, cinnamon, and baking soda and then stir until well mixed.
5. Take a separate large bowl, crack the egg in it, add sugar, oil, pumpkin puree, and beat by using an electric beater until blended.
6. Pour egg mixture into the flour mixture, stir by using a wooden spoon until incorporated and smooth batter comes together.
7. Pour half of the batter into the prepared pan, spread filling on top, cover with the batter and then bake for 1 hour to 1 hour and 10 minutes or more until the crust turned golden brown and passes the toothpick test; a toothpick should come out clean from the pan or else continue baking for another 10 minutes.
8. When done, let the bread cool in its pan for 10 minutes, then carefully lift out the bread, and transfer it to a wire rack for 1 hour or more until cooled.
9. Cut bread into twelve slices and then serve.

Orange Bread

Brighten up your gloomy winter day with a citrusy loaf of orange. Make-ahead some extra loaf and enjoy it during summer at the time of the coffee break.

Prep Time:	20 minutes	Calories:	210
Cook Time:	50 minutes	Fat (g):	10
Total Time:	1 h 10 m	Protein (g):	2
Servings:	12	Carbs:	29

Ingredients:

For the Bread:

- Butter, unsalted, softened   1/3 cup
- Sugar   ¾ cup

- Eggs, at room temperature | 2
- Orange zest | 1 ½ tablespoons
- All-purpose flour | 2 cups
- Baking soda | 1 teaspoon
- Baking powder | 1 teaspoon
- Salt | ¼ teaspoon
- Ground cinnamon | ¼ teaspoon
- Yogurt | 1 cup
- Raisins | ¼ cup

For the Glaze:
- Lemon juice | 1 teaspoon
- Orange juice | 1 teaspoon
- Powdered sugar | 1/3 cup

Instructions:

1. Switch on the oven, then set it to 350 degrees F (177°C) and let it preheat.
2. Meanwhile, take a 4-by-8 inches bread pan, grease it with oil and set it aside until required.
3. Take a large bowl, place butter in it, beat it until fluffy, beat in sugar and eggs, one at a time, until smooth and then beat in orange zest until combined.
4. Take a separate large bowl, place flour in it, add salt, cinnamon, baking powder, and soda and then stir until mixed.
5. Add yogurt into the butter mixture, beat in flour mixture, 1/3 portion at a time, until incorporated and then fold in raisins until mixed.
6. Spoon the mixture into the prepared bread pan and then bake for 50 minutes or more until the crust turned golden brown and passes the toothpick test; a toothpick should come out clean from the pan or else continue baking for another 10 minutes.
7. When done, let the bread cool in its pan for 5 minutes, then carefully lift out the bread, and transfer it to a wire rack for 30 minutes until cooled.
8. Meanwhile, prepare the glaze and for this, take a small bowl, place all the ingredients in it and then whisk until smooth.
9. Drizzle the glaze over the cooled bread, cut it into twelve slices and then serve.

Italian Sweet Bread

This golden Italian bread offer sweetness in every slice.

Prep Time:	55 minutes	Calories:	87
Cook Time:	25 minutes	Fat (g):	2
Total Time:	1 h 20 m	Protein (g):	3
Servings:	16	Carbs:	15

Ingredients:

For the Bread:

- Milk, at 80 degrees F   ½ cup

• Egg, at room temperature	½
• Butter, unsalted, softened	1 tablespoon
• Sugar	2 tablespoons
• Salt	½ teaspoon
• All-purpose flour	1 ½ cups
• Yeast, active, dry	1 teaspoon
For the Egg Wash:	
• Italian seasoning	½ teaspoon
• Water	½ tablespoon
• Egg, at room temperature	½

Instructions:

1. Take a 9 inches round pan, grease it with oil, and set it aside until required.
2. Take a large bowl, place flour in it, add remaining ingredients for the bread in it, and then whisk well by using an electric beater until incorporated and smooth batter for dough comes together.
3. Spoon the dough into the prepared bread pan, cover it with a kitchen towel and let it rest for 45 minutes or more at warm temperature until doubled in size.
4. Meanwhile, switch on the oven, then set it to 350 degrees F (177°C) and let it preheat.
5. Prepare the egg wash and for this, take a small bowl, add ½ egg in it, add water and then whisk until beaten.
6. When the dough is ready to bake, brush its top with the egg wash, sprinkle with the Italian seasoning, and then bake for 25 minutes or more until the crust turned golden brown and passes the toothpick test; a toothpick should come out clean from the pan or else continue baking for another 10 minutes.
7. When done, let the bread cool in its pan for 10 minutes, then carefully lift out the bread, and transfer it to a wire rack for 30 minutes or more until cooled.
8. Cut bread into sixteen slices and then serve.

Butter Pecan Bread

This pecan bread offers a perfect blend of nutmeg and cinnamon flavors. It is an ideal snack as well, and you can also serve it as a dessert instead of a pound cake. Slice a thick piece of this sweet bread and serve with favorite ice cream scoop.

Prep Time:	15 minutes	Calories:	171
Cook Time:	50 minutes	Fat (g):	7
Total Time:	1 h 5 m	Protein (g):	5
Servings:	10	Carbs:	21

Ingredients:

• All-purpose flour	2 ¼ cups
• Baking powder	2 teaspoons
• Baking soda	½ teaspoon
• Salt	½ teaspoon
• Ground cinnamon	½ teaspoon
• Ground nutmeg	¼ teaspoon
• Brown sugar	1 cup
• Egg, at room temperature	1
• Buttermilk	1 cup
• Butter, unsalted, melted	3 tablespoons
• Chopped pecans	1 cup

Instructions:

1. Switch on the oven, then set it to 350 degrees F (177°C) and let it preheat.
2. Meanwhile, take a 9-by-5 inches bread pan, grease it with oil and set it aside until required.
3. Take a large bowl, place flour in it, add salt, all the spices, baking soda, and powder, stir until mixed and then stir in sugar.
4. Take a small bowl, crack the egg in it, whisk in butter, and buttermilk until well blended.
5. Pour egg mixture into the mixture of flour, whisk by using an electric beater until incorporated, and then fold in pecans.
6. Spoon the dough into the prepared bread pan and then bake for 50 minutes or more until the crust turned golden brown and passes the toothpick test; a toothpick should come out clean from the pan or else continue baking for another 10 minutes.
7. When done, let the bread cool in its pan for 10 minutes, then carefully lift out the bread, and transfer it to a wire rack for 1 hour or more until cooled.
8. Cut bread into ten slices and then serve.

Cinnamon and Sugar Bread

This basic bread needs common pantry ingredients and one hour to come together. Have as a breakfast, snack, or dessert.

Prep Time:	15 minutes	Calories:	170
Cook Time:	50 minutes	Fat (g):	4
Total Time:	1 h 5 m	Protein (g):	5
Servings:	8	Carbs:	31

Ingredients:

• Sugar	1 cup + 1/3 cup
• Ground cinnamon	2 teaspoons
• All-purpose flour	2 cups
• Baking powder	1 tablespoon
• Salt	½ teaspoon
• Egg, at room temperature	1
• Raisins	½ cup
• Milk, at room temperature	1 cup
• Olive oil	1/3 cup

Instructions:

1. Switch on the oven, then set it to 350 degrees F (177°C) and let it preheat.
2. Meanwhile, take a 9-by-5 inches bread pan, grease it with oil and set it aside until required.
3. Take a large bowl, place flour in it, add salt, baking powder, and 1 cup of sugar and then stir until mixed.
4. Take a medium bowl, crack the egg in it and then beat in oil and milk until well combined.
5. Pour the egg mixture into the mixture of flour, beat until incorporated.
6. Add raisins and mix until incorporated and then pour half of the mixture into the prepared pan.
7. Stir together remaining sugar and cinnamon, sprinkle it on top of the batter into the pan, and then cover with the remaining batter.
8. Bake for 50 minutes or more until the crust turned golden brown and passes the toothpick test; a toothpick should come out clean from the pan or else continue baking for another 10 minutes.
9. When done, let the bread cool in its pan for 10 minutes, then carefully lift out the bread, and transfer it to a wire rack for 1 hour or more until cooled.
10. Cut bread into eight slices and then serve.

Bourbon Banana Bread

This banana bread recipe is amazingly delicious and unbelievably moist. The pair of banana and bourbon glaze makes the texture of this loaf moist and dense.

Prep Time:	15 minutes	Calories:	264
Cook Time:	1 hour	Fat (g):	13
Total Time:	1 h 15 m	Protein (g):	4
Servings:	12	Carbs:	29

Ingredients:

For the Bread:

- Bourbon   6 tablespoons
- All-purpose flour   1 ¼ cups

- Baking powder   2 ½ teaspoons
- Salt   ½ teaspoon
- Butter, unsalted, melted   ½ cup
- Sugar   ½ cup
- Eggs, at room temperature   2
- Bananas, mashed   3
- Vanilla extract, unsweetened   1 teaspoon

  For the Glaze:

- Bourbon   1 tablespoon
- Powdered sugar   ½ cup
- Lemon zest   1 tablespoon

Instructions:

1. Prepare the bread, and for this, take a small saucepan, place it over medium heat, pour in bourbon, heat it for 2 minutes, and then set aside until required.
2. Take a 9-by-5 inches bread pan, grease it with oil, and set it aside until required.
3. Switch on the oven, then set it to 325 degrees F (163°C) and let it preheat.
4. Take a large bowl, place flour in it, add salt and baking powder and then stir until mixed.
5. Take a large bowl, place butter in it, beat in sugar until fluffy; beat in eggs, one at a time, until blended and then beat in vanilla, bananas, and bourbon until well combined.
6. Beat in flour mixture, one-third portion at a time, until incorporated.
7. Transfer the mixture into the prepared bread pan and then bake for 1 hour or more until the crust turned golden brown and passes the toothpick test; a toothpick should come out clean from the pan or else continue baking for another 10 minutes.
8. When done, let the bread cool in its pan for 10 minutes, then carefully lift out the bread, and transfer it to a wire rack for 30 minutes or more until cooled.
9. Meanwhile, prepare the glaze and for this, take a small bowl, place bourbon and sugar in it, and then whisk until smooth.
10. Drizzle the glaze over the bread, then sprinkle some lemon zest on the top.
11. Cut bread into twelve slices and then serve.

Spring Sweet Bread

Incorporate all the spring flavors in one bread. It is tasty and tender and amazing to eat.
With the sweet topping, it makes a perfect dessert treat and giveaway gift.

Prep Time:	3 h 15 m	Calories:	195
Cook Time:	30 minutes	Fat (g):	7
Total Time:	3 h 45 m	Protein (g):	4
Servings:	12	Carbs:	29

Ingredients:

For the Bread:

• Butter, unsalted	2 tablespoons
• Milk, at room temperature	½ cup
• All-purpose flour	2 cups
• Yeast, active, dry	1 teaspoon

- Sugar — 3 tablespoons
- Salt — ½ teaspoon
- Egg, at room temperature — 1
- Vanilla extract, unsweetened — ½ teaspoon
- Dried fruit mixture — ½ cup

  For the Topping:
- Sugar — 2 tablespoons
- All-purpose flour — 2 ½ tablespoons
- Butter, unsalted — 1 tablespoon
- Egg white, at room temperature — 1

Instructions:

1. Take a large bowl, pour in the milk, and then whisk in butter until combined.
2. Add remaining ingredients for the bread in it, except for the dried fruits, and then stir well by using a wooden spoon until incorporated and smooth batter comes together.
3. Knead in dried fruits, cover the bowl with a kitchen towel and let the dough rest for 1 hour and 30 minutes at a warm place until doubled in size.
4. Then punch in the dough, transfer it into a 9-by-5 inches bread pan, cover it with a kitchen towel and let it rest for 1 hour and 30 minutes at a warm place.
5. Meanwhile, switch on the oven, then set it to 350 degrees F (177°C) and let it pre-heat.
6. Prepare the topping and for this, take a small bowl, place sugar, flour, and butter in it and then stir well until mixture resembles crumbs.
7. Place egg white in a small bowl, beat well, brush it on top of the prepared dough, and then spread the topping on it.
8. Bake for 30 minutes or more until the crust turned golden brown and passes the toothpick test; a toothpick should come out clean from the pan or else continue baking for another 10 minutes.
9. When done, carefully lift out the bread and transfer it to a wire rack for 1 hour or more until cooled.
10. Cut bread into twelve slices and then serve.

Chocolate Chip Zucchini Bread

Prep Time:	15 minutes	Calories:	151
Cook Time:	1 h 10 m	Fat (g):	8
Total Time:	1 h 25 m	Protein (g):	2
Servings:	12	Carbs:	19

Ingredients:

- All-purpose flour   1 ¾ cups
- Baking soda   ¾ teaspoon

- Baking powder — ½ teaspoon
- Cocoa powder, unsweetened — ¼ cup
- Ground cinnamon — 1 teaspoon
- Salt — ½ teaspoon
- Eggs, at room temperature — 2
- Sugar — 1 cup
- Olive oil — 1/2 cup
- Vanilla extract, unsweetened — 1 teaspoon
- Shredded zucchini — 1 cup
- Chocolate chips, semisweet — 1 ½ cups + 2 tablespoons (for toppings)

Instructions:

1. Switch on the oven, then set it to 350 degrees F (177°C) and let it preheat.
2. Meanwhile, take a 9-by-5 inches bread pan, grease it with oil and set it aside until required.
3. Take a large bowl, place flour in it, add salt, cinnamon, cocoa powder, baking powder, and baking soda and then stir until mixed.
4. Take a separate large bowl, crack the eggs in it, beat in sugar by using an electric beater until smooth, and then beat in vanilla and oil until combined.
5. Stir flour mixture into the egg mixture, one-third portion at a time, and then fold in chocolate chips and zucchini until just mixed.
6. Spoon the dough into the prepared bread pan and then bake for 1 hour and 10 minutes or more until the crust turned golden brown and passes the toothpick test; a toothpick should come out clean from the pan or else continue baking for another 10 minutes.
7. When done, let the bread cool in its pan for 10 minutes, then top it with some extra chocolate chips and carefully lift out the bread, and transfer it to a wire rack for 1 hour or more until cooled.
8. Cut bread into twelve slices and then serve.

Brown Sugar Coconut Bread

This no-yeast sweet bread is incredibly easy to make and flavorsome.

Prep Time:	15 minutes	Calories:	121
Cook Time:	40 minutes	Fat (g):	2
Total Time:	55 minutes	Protein (g):	3
Servings:	12	Carbs:	21

Ingredients:

• Brown sugar	1 cup
• All-purpose flour	2 cups
• Salt	½ teaspoon
• Baking powder	1 tablespoon
• Coconut flakes	¼ cup
• Eggs, at room temperature	1
• Milk	1 cup
• Olive oil	5 tablespoons
• Bananas, mashed	2
• Oats	3 tablespoons

Instructions:

1. Switch on the oven, then set it to 350 degrees F (177°C) and let it preheat.
2. Meanwhile, take a 9-by-5 inches bread pan, grease it with oil and set it aside until required.
3. Take a large bowl, place flour in it, add salt, sugar, coconut flakes, and baking powder, and then stir until mixed.
4. Take a separate large bowl, crack the egg in it and then beat in oil and milk by using an electric beater until blended.
5. Beat in flour mixture, one-third portion at a time, until incorporated, stir in bananas, transfer the mixture into the prepared bread pan and then sprinkle oats on top.
6. Bake for 40 minutes or more until the crust turned golden brown and passes the toothpick test; a toothpick should come out clean from the pan or else continue baking for another 10 minutes.
7. When done, let the bread cool in its pan for 10 minutes, then carefully lift out the bread, and transfer it to a wire rack for 1 hour or more until cooled.
8. Cut bread into twelve slices and then serve.

Cranberry Orange Bread

One word for this bread – heavenly! This beautiful loaf offers a perfect blend of the sweet and tangy flavor of orange and cranberries. And, its smell is enough to entice anyone to eat it. You can also turn up this recipe into muffins.

Prep Time:	20 minutes	Calories:	222
Cook Time:	30 minutes	Fat (g):	11
Total Time:	50 minutes	Protein (g):	4
Servings:	12	Carbs:	27

Ingredients:

<u>For the Bread:</u>

- All-purpose flour   1 ½ cups

- Baking powder — 2 ½ teaspoons
- Sugar — ½ cup
- Salt — ¼ teaspoon
- Butter, unsalted, melted — 6 tablespoons
- Egg, at room temperature — 1
- Whole milk, at room temperature — ¾ cup
- Sour cream — ½ cup
- Vanilla extract, unsweetened — ¼ teaspoon
- Orange juice — ¼ cup
- Orange zest — 4 tablespoons
- Cranberries, fresh — ¼ cup

Instructions:

1. Switch on the oven, then set it to 450 degrees F (232°C) and let it preheat.
2. Meanwhile, take a 9-by-5 inches bread pan, grease it with oil and set it aside until required.
3. Take a large bowl, place flour in it, add salt, sugar, and baking powder, and then stir until mixed.
4. Take a separate large bowl, place butter in it, and then beat in remaining ingredients except for berries until smooth.
5. Beat in flour mixture, one-third portion at a time, until incorporated and then fold in cranberries until just mixed.
6. Spoon the batter into the prepared bread pan and then bake for 30 minutes or more until the crust turned golden brown and passes the toothpick test; a toothpick should come out clean from the pan or else continue baking for another 10 minutes.
7. When done, let the bread cool in its pan for 10 minutes, then carefully lift out the bread, and transfer it to a wire rack for 30 minutes or more until cooled.
8. Cut it into twelve slices and then serve.

Molasses Sweet Bread

It is perfect for a breakfast toast, brunch, or sandwiches.

Prep Time:	4 h 15 m	Calories:	142
Cook Time:	40 minutes	Fat (g):	1
Total Time:	4 h 55 m	Protein (g):	3
Servings:	10	Carbs:	30

Ingredients:

- Oats   ½ cup
- Butter, unsalted   ¾ tablespoon
- Yeast, dry, active   1 teaspoon

- Molasses ¼ cup
- Salt 1 teaspoon
- Whole-wheat flour 1 cup
- All-purpose flour 2 cups
- Water, warm ½ cup
- Water, boiling 2 cups

Instructions:

1. Take a large bowl, place oats in it, add butter, pour in boiling water, and let the mixture rest for 1 hour until oats have softened.
2. Then take a small bowl, place yeast in it, pour in warm water, stir and let the mixture rest for 5 minutes until emulsified.
3. Add yeast mixture into the oats along with salt and molasses, stir until combined and then stir in whole-wheat flour and all-purpose flour, ½ cup at a time, until incorporated and the dough comes together.
4. Spoon the dough onto a clean working space dusted with flour and then knead it for 5 minutes.
5. Take a large bowl, grease it with oil, place dough in it, brush the top with oil, cover with the kitchen towel and let it rest for 1 hour and 30 minutes at the warm place until doubled in size.
6. Then punch down the dough, place it in 9-by-5 inches greased bread pan, cover the top with a kitchen towel and let it rest for another 1 hour and 30 minutes.
7. Meanwhile, switch on the oven, then set it to 375 degrees F (190°C) and let it preheat.
8. Then bake the bread for 40 minutes or more until the crust turned deep brown and passes the toothpick test; a toothpick should come out clean from the pan or else continue baking for another 10 minutes.
9. When done, let the bread cool in its pan for 10 minutes, then carefully lift out the bread, and transfer it to a wire rack for 1 hour or more until cooled.
10. Cut bread into ten slices and then serve.

Sweet Potato Bread

This recipe presents old-fashion sweet potato bread in a new light. It is comforting and delicious, and the best way to incorporate leftover sweet potatoes into your diet.

Prep Time:	15 minutes	Calories:	328
Cook Time:	1 h 10 m	Fat (g):	12
Total Time:	1 h 25 m	Protein (g):	4
Servings:	10	Carbs:	51

Ingredients:

- Sweet potatoes, canned
  15 oz (425 g) + 2 tablespoons liquid reserved

- Sugar
  1 ¼ cups

- Water, warm — 1/3 cup
- Olive oil — 1/3 cup
- Eggs, at room temperature — 2
- All-purpose flour — 1 ¾ cups
- Baking soda — 1 teaspoon
- Salt — ¾ teaspoon
- Nutmeg — ½ teaspoon
- Baking powder — ¼ teaspoon
- Chopped pecans — ½ cup
- Allspice — ½ teaspoon
- Ground cinnamon — 1 teaspoon

Instructions:

1. Switch on the oven, then set it to 350 degrees F (177°C) and let it preheat.
2. Meanwhile, take a 9-by-5 inches bread pan, grease it with oil and set it aside until required.
3. Take a large bowl, place sweet potatoes in it, add its liquid along with sugar, eggs, oil, and water, and then beat until well mixed.
4. Take a separate large bowl, place flour in it, add salt, cinnamon, nutmeg, all-spices, baking powder, and soda and then stir until mixed.
5. Stir the mixture of flour into the sweet potato mixture until incorporated and then fold in pecans.
6. Spoon the mixture into the prepared bread pan and then bake for 1 hour and 10 minutes or more until the crust turned golden brown and passes the tooth-pick test; a toothpick should come out clean from the pan or else continue baking for another 10 minutes.
7. When done, let the bread cool in its pan for 10 minutes, then carefully lift out the bread, and transfer it to a wire rack for 30 minutes or more until cooled.
8. Cut bread into ten slices and then serve.

Sweet Potato Bread with Pecans and Fruits

Another recipe to take classic sweet potato bread to another level. It is super easy to prepare and bake. It includes spices, chopped pecans, fruits, and apple sauce. Feel free to replace pecans with dried cranberries or chocolate chips.

Prep Time:	15 minutes	Calories:	267
Cook Time:	1h 10 m	Fat (g):	11
Total Time:	1 h 25 m	Protein (g):	5
Servings:	12	Carbs:	39

Ingredients:

• All-purpose flour	1 ½ cups
• Baking powder	2 teaspoons
• Salt	¼ teaspoon
• Ground nutmeg	1 teaspoon
• Ground cinnamon	½ teaspoon
• Sugar	1 cup
• Chopped pecans	1 cup
• Chopped dried fruits (desired)	½ cup
• Eggs, at room temperature	2
• Applesauce, unsweetened	½ cup
• Milk, at room temperature	4 tablespoons
• Sweet potatoes, cooked, mashed	1 cup

Instructions:

1. Switch on the oven, then set it to 325 degrees F (163°C) and let it preheat.
2. Meanwhile, take a 9-by-5 inches bread pan, grease it with oil and set it aside until required.
3. Take a large bowl, place flour in it, add salt, all spices, baking powder, sugar, fruits, and pecans and then stir until mixed.
4. Take a separate bowl, crack the eggs in it, beat in mashed sweet potatoes, milk, and applesauce until smooth and then beat in flour mixture, one-third portion at a time, until incorporated.
5. Spoon the mixture into the prepared bread pan and then bake for 1 hour and 10 minutes or more until the crust turned golden brown and passes the toothpick test; a toothpick should come out clean from the pan or else continue baking for another 10 minutes.
6. When done, let the bread cool in its pan for 10 minutes, then carefully lift out the bread, and transfer it to a wire rack for 30 minutes or more until cooled.
7. Cut bread into twelve slices and then serve.

Pineapple Nut Bread with Cinnamon

This sweet and nutty bread loaded with pineapple will become your family favorite.

Prep Time:	15 minutes	Calories:	319
Cook Time:	60 minutes	Fat (g):	19
Total Time:	1 h 15 m	Protein (g):	5
Servings:	12	Carbs:	34

Ingredients:

For the Bread:

- Brown sugar   ¾ cup

- Butter, unsalted, softened   6 tablespoons
- Eggs, at room temperature   2
- Crushed pineapple, undrained   8 oz (227 g)
- Vanilla extract, unsweetened   1 teaspoon
- Chopped walnuts   1 cup
- All-purpose flour   2 ¼ cups
- Baking powder   2 teaspoons
- Baking soda   ¼ teaspoon
- Salt   ¼ teaspoon

For the Topping:

- Sugar   1 tablespoon
- Ground cinnamon   ¼ teaspoon
- Chopped walnuts   ¼ cup

Instructions:

1. Switch on the oven, then set it to 350 degrees F (177°C) and let it preheat.
2. Meanwhile, take a 9-by-5 inches bread pan, grease it with oil and set it aside until required.
3. Prepare the bread and for this, take a large bowl, place butter in it, cream together the brown sugar, and then beat in eggs, one at a time, until blended.
4. Add vanilla, walnuts, and undrained pineapples and then stir until mixed.
5. Take a separate large bowl, place flour in it, add salt, baking powder, and soda, stir until combined, and then stir this mixture into the egg mixture until incorporated and smooth batter comes together.
6. Spoon the batter into the prepared bread pan, then stir together all the ingredients for the toppings and spread on top of bread batter.
7. Bake for 50 to 60 minutes or more until the crust turned golden brown and passes the toothpick test; a toothpick should come out clean from the pan or else continue baking for another 10 minutes.
8. When done, let the bread cool in its pan for 10 minutes, then carefully lift out the bread, and transfer it to a wire rack for 30 minutes or more until cooled.
9. Cut bread into twelve slices and then serve.

Trinidad Coconut Sweet Bread

This coconut bread is so fantastic that you will have another slice after the first one. It is loaded with dried fruits, raisins, and spices. Eat it along or have it as a sandwich with a favorite spread.

Prep Time:	15 minutes	Calories:	252
Cook Time:	45 minutes	Fat (g):	5
Total Time:	60 minutes	Protein (g):	3
Servings:	12	Carbs:	48

Ingredients:

For the Bread:

- Coconut, dry   ½
- Water   ½ cup
- All-purpose flour   3 cups
- Baking powder   3 teaspoons
- Sugar   1 cup

- Butter, unsalted, softened   2 oz (57 g)
- Raisins   ½ cup
- Dried fruits   ¼ cup
- Chopped cherries   ¼ cup
- Mixed peel   1/3 cup
- Ground cinnamon   ½ teaspoon
- Nutmeg   ½ teaspoon
- Coconut essence, unsweetened   ½ teaspoon

  For Glaze:
- Water   1 tablespoon
- Lime juice   1 tablespoon
- Honey   1 tablespoon

Instructions:

1. Switch on the oven, then set it to 350 degrees F (177°C) and let it preheat.
2. Meanwhile, take a 9-by-5 inches bread pan, grease it with oil and set it aside until required.
3. Remove flesh from the coconut, cut it into small pieces and then place it into a food processor.
4. Pour in water, pulse for 1 to 2 minutes until blended, and then pour the mixture into a large bowl.
5. Add flour, sugar, baking powder, and butter, stir until mixed, then add remaining ingredients for the bread in it and stir until incorporated and smooth batter for the dough comes together.
6. Spoon the batter into the prepared bread pan and then bake for 45 minutes or more until the crust turned golden brown and passes the toothpick test; a toothpick should come out clean from the pan or else continue baking for another 10 minutes.
7. When done, let the bread cool in its pan for 10 minutes, then carefully lift out the bread, and transfer it to a wire rack for 30 minutes or more until cooled.
8. Meanwhile, prepare the glaze and for this, take a small bowl, add all of its ingredients in it and then stir until well combined.
9. Drizzle the glaze on top of the bread, cut it into twelve slices, and then serve.

Date Nut Bread

Prep Time:	15 minutes	Calories:	204
Cook Time:	45 minutes	Fat (g):	7
Total Time:	1 hour	Protein (g):	4
Servings:	8	Carbs:	31

Ingredients:

- Water, boiling   1 cup
- Dates, chopped   8 oz (227 g)
- Butter, unsalted   2 tablespoons
- Sugar   ¾ cup

- Brown sugar   ¼ cup
- Egg, at room temperature   1
- All-purpose flour   2 ¼ cups
- Baking powder   1 tablespoon
- Salt   ½ teaspoon
- Walnuts, chopped   ½ cup

Instructions:

1. Switch on the oven, then set it to 350 degrees F (177°C) and let it preheat.
2. Meanwhile, take a 9-by-5 inches bread pan, grease it with oil and set it aside until required.
3. Take a medium bowl, place chopped dates in it, pour in water, add butter, and then put it aside until required.
4. Take a large bowl, beat the brown sugar, sugar, and the egg with a mixer until light.
5. Take a separate large bowl, place flour in it, add salt and baking powder and then stir until mixed.
6. Beat flour mixture into the butter mixture, one-third of the portion at a time, along with date mixture until incorporated and then fold in nuts until mixed.
7. Spoon the batter into the prepared bread pan and then bake for 45 minutes or more until the crust turned golden brown and passes the toothpick test; a toothpick should come out clean from the pan or else continue baking for another 10 minutes.
8. When done, let the bread cool in its pan for 10 minutes, then carefully lift out the bread, and transfer it to a wire rack for 1 hour or more until cooled.
9. Cut bread into eight slices and then serve.

Printed by Amazon Italia Logistica S.r.l.
Torrazza Piemonte (TO), Italy

16459053R00069